# Faraci's SAT
# Math Survival Guide

By Michael Faraci

# Acknowledgements

I want to thank everyone who helped me in putting the project together. Angela Tartaro for her editing insights, Michael Massa for the cover design and all the students who helped out with their suggestions.  Most of all to my family who put up with me while I worked on this.

Lauren Saez
54c

Averages
Compl. fig
Functions
Linear Graphs
Logic
Probability
Permutations
Polygons
Solids
Sequences
Triangles

Angles
Compl fig
Equations
Functions
Data Analysis
Linear Graphs
Logic
Probability
# properties
%
Permutations
Polygons
Solids
Sequences
Sets

The SAT is a trademark of the College Entrance Exam Board who was not involved in any way, and does not endorse, this book.

# Table of Contents

## Note from the Author

When I began creating this workbook, I wanted a resource that would help me teach the SAT in the order that made sense mathematically and that worked with my style of teaching. It was a huge task because as soon as I would add one topic or section , I realized there was a need for another section. Eventually, I realized that the finished product could be more than just a resource for me to teach. It had become a great workbook to help students study and learn. Every section is organized the way a class should be organized. First, you start with introductory problems in order from easy to hard. Next there is a lesson explaining relevant facts. Finally, a section with practice problems involving the topics you have just learned. The practice sections all begin with basic problems that don't have any twists to them and then progress into a "SAT" style questions.

Be aware that most of the "SAT style" questions in this book are medium to difficult . Don't panic when earlier questions seem difficult. I would rather my students see harder questions when they practice so that they are not so hard when they see the same concepts on the actual test. I have found this "practice hard, test easy" approach best.

As you're practicing and studying for the exam, realize that there is a difference between the math you are doing in your schools and "SAT" math. There are some techniques and strategies you will apply to the SAT that you would not use in your math class. Keep in mind that the mathematical principles are the same. No amount of SAT practice will replace solid mathematical skills. Ideally you will need both.

Finally, keep in mind that you will get out of this book (and any other test preparation) exactly what you put into it. You can't expect to start working on this one week before the exam and improve. Life doesn't work that way and neither does the SAT. Be sure to   practice with actual exams in the "10 Real SAT's" book and to time yourself as you go. Over time and with practice you will see improvement.

Good Luck!!

# Knowing the Test

The first step in improving your score is to know how the test is made up and how it is scored. You will have 3 math sections counted toward your score. There may be a 4th section which is an experimental section. This is explained on page 5.

Section 1                                                          25 Minutes
20 Multiple Choice Questions


Section 2                                                          25 Minutes
8 Multiple Choice Questions
10 Grid In Questions

Section 3                                                          20 Minutes
16 Multiple Choice Questions

The way the test is scored is unlike any other test you take in high school. On the multiple choice questions you will get one point for every right answer and you will lose 1/4 point for every wrong answer. Omitted questions don't get or lose anything. For the grid ins you will get one point for each right answer but *you won't lose anything for wrong answers*. For this reason, you should never omit a grid in question. The only exception to this rule is for questions where you don't have a clue and it will take too much time to make a good guess.

(# M.C. Correct)-1/4(# M.C Wrong)+(# Correct Grid Ins)=Raw Score

If the raw score is not a whole number, standard rounding rules apply. A raw score of 35.25 will be considered a 35 and a score of 35.5 will be considered a 36. This is why wrong answers can hurt so much.

The fact that omitted questions aren't counted as wrong is very important. <u>You have to know when to answer and also when not to answer.</u>

# **Frequently Asked Questions**

## **When should I guess?**

The fact that each multiple choice question has 5 choices and you lose 1/4 point for wrong answers is not a coincidence. There is a 1 in 5 chance of guessing correctly and you will lose 1/4 of a point for guessing incorrectly. The risk outweighs the reward. You can guess on multiple choice questions if you can successfully eliminate choices. Probability says if you can eliminate just one choice you should guess. In order for this to work, however, you would have to guess a lot. A better rule is to eliminate 2 choices. If 2 choices are eliminated, you would have a 1/3 chance of guessing correctly. Supposing you were guessing on 3 questions, probability says that you would get 1 correct and 2 of them incorrect. Look at what it would do to your raw score:

$$1 \text{ correct} - 1/4(2 \text{ incorrect}) = +1/2$$

It would add a 1/2 point to your raw score. With rounding rules, this could be like adding a point.

Bottom Line: If you can eliminate 2 choices then guess. Otherwise, omit the question.

## **What calculator should I use?**

You can use almost any calculator you want on the exam. The only ones that are not allowed are laptop computers and anything that makes noise. You will NOT be allowed to use the calculator on your cell phone . I would recommend the TI-84 or some similar graphing calculator. Make sure that you are familiar with your calculator. Be careful of higher end calculators that are not user friendly or that you simply don't know how to use. It doesn't matter what the calculator can do if you don't know how to use it.

Make sure that your calculator is set up correctly and replace the batteries before the test.

## **How long is the test?**

The total time will be a little over 4 hours. You'll be given 2 short breaks so be sure to bring a snack. Don't bring a candy bar. You'll have a sugar high and then a sugar crash!

## **When should I start preparing?**

This one depends on what type of student you are. I find that 2 to 3 months of preparation is perfect. The idea is to be peaking at just the right time. Eventually there will be diminishing returns. If you are an average student and got a 51 on the PSAT, don't think that working for a year is going to get you to that 800 on the test. Have appropriate goals.

## **When should I take the test?**

Again, this depends on what type of a student you are and what your schedule is like. Due to AP exams, many students elect to take the test before May. Before May, the test is offered in December, January, and March. Make sure to decide which SAT II exams you are going to take and when. If you are an average student and are not accelerated, the May or June exam is probably best choice for you. By then you should have finished enough of your high schools' math curriculum and there won't be any gaps in what you should know.

## What does "Score Choice" mean?

Score choice is the College Board's attempt at reducing stress for the students. You have the choice to release your test scores or to not release them. Some schools will require you to release all your scores. Be sure to check with the schools you are applying to and/or your schools' guidance counselor.

## Can I mix and match scores from different sections?

Just as in score choice, schools set their own policies. Some look at the single best total score and some will allow you to mix and match sections from different tests. Again, check with the schools you are applying to and/or your schools' guidance counselor.

## How many times should I take the test?

The College Board will let you take it as many times as you want . But the question is: Why are you taking it so many times? Most students take it twice. Once during their junior year and once, if necessary, in the beginning of their senior year. Unless there are extenuating circumstances (i.e. you took it when you were very sick) this is probably all that is necessary.

## What math is on the test?

Most of the math is from the first few years of your high school curriculum. Many topics include basic arithmetic and number facts. Always keep in mind that the SAT is given every year to selected middle school students. These students have the necessary tools to do the work. If you are using advanced topics to answer questions (logarithms, derivatives, Law of Sines/Cosines, trigonometric identities, etc... ) then you are approaching the problem the wrong way.

## What should I bring the day of the test?

Be at your test center 15 minutes before the time indicated on your admission ticket. You should have with you the following items:
1. Your admission ticket
2. Photo ID (driver's license, school ID, valid passport)
3. Several sharpened #2 pencils with erasers
4. Calculator (be sure to have new batteries!!)
5. A watch, just in case you can't see the clock in the room
6. A sensible snack for the breaks

## What is the experimental section?

The College Board inserts one extra section onto every SAT exam. This section is used to develop questions that will be on future tests. The experimental section is never scored but it is also never labeled. NEVER try to guess which one is the experimental section. Do every section. Treat every section the same way.

# Setting Your Goals

Setting an appropriate goal is the first step in successful preparation. If you got a 51 on the math section of the PSAT (equivalent to a 510 on the SAT) don't think you can work an extra couple of months and get an 800. My standard is to raise your PSAT score 50 to 100 points regardless of whether you thought your PSAT score was good for was accurate or not. If you had a really bad day and got a 51 on the PSAT but you are in all upper level classes and an A math student, start out with a goal of 610. If 51 was about right for you, set your goal for 560.

The goal you set is flexible. As you work, you should be taking practice tests each week (get the "10 Real SAT's" book published by The College Board). If you find yourself reaching your goal or higher on two consecutive practice tests, raise your goal.

# Strategy

Your goal will determine how many questions you are going to answer on each page. The only way you should ever answer all of the questions is if your goal was to get a top score of 700 or higher. However, even if you are attempting to get a perfect score and you come to a difficult question you should only guess if you can safely eliminate 2 choices. If not, you're better off omitting the question. There have been instances where a perfect score was attained with a raw score of 53 out of 54.

Skipping some of the questions at the end of a section achieves two goals:

      1. You are avoiding the questions that you are most likely to get wrong.
      2. You are allowing yourself more time to answer the other questions.

The time factor is huge. Over the course of the test, you will take 54 questions in a total of 70 minutes. This is an average of about 1 minute 18 seconds per question. Some of the later questions are more difficult and therefore will take more time. By skipping these questions, you can spend more time on the questions that you have a higher probability of getting right.

## A Tale of Two Testers

The two testers below both got the same number of questions right (60% on each section). The difference was that one stopped where they should have and the other tried to answer all of the questions. Look at the difference in their raw scores.

|  | Tester 1(Ben) | Tester 2(Jerry) |
|---|---|---|
| M.C. Right | 33 | 33 |
| M.C. Wrong | 0 | 15 |
| Grid In Right | 6 | 6 |
| **Raw Score** | 39 | 35.25=35 |
| **Scaled Score** | 620* | 580* |

Both testers had the same number of correct answers, Jerry however, made the mistake of answering every question. Because he got so many questions wrong, it lowered his point total by 40 points.

# Have a Plan

The following strategies offer guidelines on how many questions you need to answer on each section in order to achieve your goal. Section 1 refers to the 20 question multiple choice section, Section 2 is the section with the 8 multiple choice and 10 grid in questions and Section 3 is the section with 16 multiple choice question sections.

The idea is to get as many questions right in the beginning of each section. By omitting the most difficult questions, you will have more time to focus on the earlier question and avoid careless mistakes. Don't be afraid to modify your strategy as you practice. Keep in mind that no matter where the question is, if you can eliminate 2 or more choices, then guess.

## Goal: 500(Answer the following)          Raw Score: Approximately 26

Section 1: 1-12
Section 2: 1-5; 9-14
Section 3: 1-10

Here you are answering a total of 33 questions so there is some room for error. The idea is to focus on the earlier questions where you have the highest chance of getting the answer correct. Avoid the later questions that are more difficult.

## Goal: 550(Answer the following)          Raw Score: Approximately 31

Section 1: 1-14
Section 2: 1-6; 9-14
Section 3: 1-12

This is a big jump in raw score and you will only be doing 5 extra questions, so you have less margin for error. Again, unless you are absolutely sure of them, skip the last questions in each section.

## Goal: 600(Answer the following)          Raw Score: Approximately 37

Section 1: 1-16
Section 2: 1-6; 9-16
Section 3: 1-12

Another big jump in raw score. Doing a total of 42 question gives you some margin for error. Keep in mind that you are still omitting a total of 12 questions here.

## Goal: 650(Answer the following)          Raw Score: Approximately 43

Section 1: 1-18
Section 2: 1-7; 9-17
Section 3: 1-14

You're now at the point where you are looking at all of the questions. Don't be afraid of any question. Following these conditions, you are skipping 6 questions and you can still get 4 questions wrong for a raw score of 43.

## Goal: 700 and above          Raw Score: Approx. 48 and up

Do every question.

# Test Taking Strategies

Here's the deal—the SAT is not interested in testing your ability in math. They're trying to test your thinking ability. Very little of the math you've learned since 9th grade is on the test. The trick is trying to get through the traps that make you take too much time.
Here are a few strategies that will help:

*DON'T read the instructions!! You've been taking practice questions while you've been preparing. The instructions will be identical to the practice exams you have already taken. Go straight to the problems and save time.

*DO READ THE QUESTIONS CAREFULLY!! Make sure you are answering what is being asked.

*Do the problems on each page, then enter in the answers on the answer sheet before going on to the next page.

*If you don't know the answer to a problem, try to eliminate choices that you know are wrong, then guess. If you can't eliminate any choices, omit the question.

The questions are usually presented in order of difficulty. The easier questions are in the beginning of each section and they get progressively more difficult. Since they are all worth the same point value, make sure you go in numberical order.

**Examples of easy, medium and hard questions are on the following page.**

# Easy-Medium-Hard Questions

Remember you are not just fighting the test, you are also fighting the clock. You must average just over 1 minute per question throughout the math section. Because of this, it is important for you to understand that the questions in the beginning of each section will usually be the easier questions. They should be done the quickest (but not so quickly that you make careless mistakes) and there will not be traps. The medium questions will be more difficult but will not have traps. The hardest questions will not only be difficult but will also have traps in them. These are usually the last few questions in each section. Try to do the following three questions in three and a half minutes.

## Easy

1. If $x+5=7$, what is the value of $3x+15$?

    a. 7
    b. 10
    c. 14
    d. 21
    e. 49

## Medium

2. If $x-7=2y$ and $x=5+3y$ , what is the value of $y$?

    a. -5
    b. -2
    c. 2
    d. 5
    e. 12

## Hard

3. Rectangle ABCD is drawn where E is the midpoint of AB. If the area of quadrilateral EBCD is 2/3, what was the area of ABCD?

    a. ½
    b. ¾
    c. 8/9
    d. 1
    e. 8/3

***Solutions to these questions are on the next page***

# Solutions

## Easy

### 1. **21**

You could solve the equation for x very quickly, but notice that $3(x+5)=3x+15$. Therefore, you could just multiply $(3)(7)$ to get 21. Very often you will have to solve for the expression, not necessarily the variable.

## Medium

### 2. **c**

You are being given two equations here.

$$x-7=2y \quad (1)$$
$$x=5+3y \quad (2)$$

By substituting equation 2 into equation 1 you get the equation

$$(5+3y)-7=2y \text{ Now solve.}$$
$$y=2$$

## Hard

### 3. **c**

Draw out rectangle ABCD with point E and connect point E to D to form trapezoid DEBC. If you then draw lines from E and B to the midpoint of CD you will get the picture below

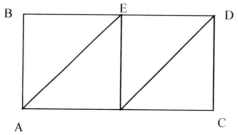

This forms 4 congruent triangles since 3 of the triangles have an area of 2/3, then you could find the area of all 4 by using the proportion:

$$\frac{3}{2/3} = \frac{4}{x}$$

$$X=8/9$$

***Keep in mind that, even if you didn't see how to solve the problem, you could have easily eliminated two of the choices. Choice A can be eliminated because it is too low

$(1/2<2/3)$ and choice E can be eliminated because it is too high . Remember that $8/3 = 2\frac{2}{3}$

# Testing Tactics

*As you prepare for the test, you are going to notice that some tactics will work on one question but not on others. It is important to get a feel for which tactics work most often and when to use them. If you try one tactic and it doesn't work, you should try something else. These are some of the more common tactics. Try to use them throughout this book.*

1. On multiple choice questions, know which choice to start with. Since over 80% of the test will be multiple choice, these are the most important questions to master. Remember that the correct answer will always be one of the choices. Possible tactics are:
   - a. Eliminating choices
   - b. Plugging in numbers for variables.
   - c. Trial and error. When doing trial and error, remember that the choices are listed in order from low to high. Therefore, start with C. If this number is too high, you can also eliminate D and E. If too low, eliminate A and B.
   - d. Make lists/charts/tables. The choices are listed vertically. You can easily make charts and lists to test out the choices.

2. Draw diagrams if the question doesn't give you one.

3. If a diagram is provided it will be drawn to scale, unless otherwise indicated.

4. When the picture is "Not drawn to scale" you can't trust it at all. Often it will help to redraw you picture and exaggerate it.

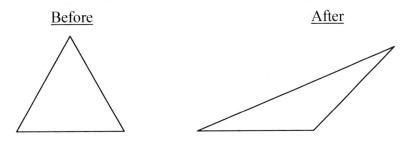

Before                    After

5. Add lines to diagrams when appropriate.

6. Subtract to find shaded regions.

7. Don't try to do extra. Very often you will end up wasting time by doing too much. For example, if the question states that $2x+3y=7$ and then asks for the value of $4x^2+12xy+9y^2$, don't try to solve for the variables. Solve for the expression!! $4x^2+12xy+9y^2=(2x+3y)^2$. Therefore, your answer would be 49.

8. Watch out for units. This is a popular trap, especially on questions that deal with perimeter, area or volume. Often, information will be given in one unit (feet) and then the question will be asking for another (inches).

9. Use your calculator as much as you can but also know when not to use it.

10. Trust charts, graphs, and grids. These are the same as diagrams in that they are always drawn to scale.

11. Look for patterns. If a problem is looking for the 83$^{rd}$ term is a sequence, you don't want to have to find the first 82 terms. Learn to recognize time traps!

12. Don't do big problems. Try to break them down into smaller problems. If a question calls for a set of 11 different numbers, it is a time trap. Use a smaller, more manageable set and see if you can get the answer that way.

It's important to note that as you practice you will see that often there are many ways to do a problem. There is not always a "best way" to do a problem. The "best way" is the way that you are most comfortable with and that gets you the correct answer in the shortest time! Keep an open mind and don't be afraid to ask your friends and classmates questions. They might have seen or figured out a way to do a problem that you haven't.

# SAT Tactics: Picking Numbers

Often, questions will give you variables and not numbers to work with. When this happens, substitute a number for each of the variables and find the solution. Then, test each choice. Picking good numbers will be very important.

1. If the length of a rectangle were increased by 30% and the width were decreased by 30%, then the area of the rectangle:

    a. remains the same

    b. increases by 10%

    c. decreases by 9%

    d. increases by 9%

    e. decreases by 10%

1. _____

2. If N candy bars cost P dollars, then how many dollars would Q candy bars cost?

    a. $\dfrac{NP}{Q}$

    b. $\dfrac{NQ}{P}$

    c. $\dfrac{PQ}{N}$

    d. $\dfrac{N}{PQ}$

    e. $\dfrac{P}{NQ}$

2. _____

3. Tom is saving S dollars every week. In T weeks, he saves K dollars. What is the value of T in terms of K and S?

    a. $SK$

    b. $S + K$

    c. $\dfrac{S}{K}$

    d. $\dfrac{K}{S}$

    e. $\dfrac{K}{S + K}$

3. _____

4. Which of the following is equivalent to $\left(3x + \dfrac{1}{3x}\right)^2 - \left(\dfrac{1}{3x} - 3x\right)^2$ ?

4. _____

      *a.* 0

      *b.* 4

      *c.* $9x^2$

      *d.* $\dfrac{1}{9x^2} + 9x^2$

      *e.* $\dfrac{1}{9x^2} + 6x + 9x^2$

5. There are 75 more boys than girls at Manhasset High School. If there are N boys, then in terms of N, what percent of students enrolled are boys?

5. _____

      *a.* $\dfrac{N}{N-75}\%$

      *b.* $\dfrac{N}{2N-75}\%$

      *c.* $\dfrac{N}{100(2N-75)}\%$

      *d.* $\dfrac{100N}{N-75}\%$

      *e.* $\dfrac{100N}{2N-75}\%$

***Solutions to this section can be found on page 143***

# SAT Tactics: Using Choices

The advantage of multiple choice questions is that the answer is always right in front of you. A good test taker will save time by testing the choices. Remember that the choices are in order from low to high. Because of this, you should always test choice C first. If its too high, you can eliminate D and E too. If it's too low, you can eliminate A and B

1. On a certain bridge, there is a toll of $3 for cars and $5 for trucks. From 50
   vehicles, all either cars or trucks, a total of $190 in tolls was collected . How
   many of the vehicles were cars?
   a. 15
   b. 20
   c. 25
   d. 30
   e. 35

   1. _____

2. The equation $(x-3)^2=2(3-x)$ is true for which of the following?
   a. 1 only
   b. 1 and 3
   c. -1 and -3
   d. 1 and -3
   e. None of the above

   2. _____

3. During a vacation Evan spent twice as much as Sean who spent three times
   as much as Ryan. If Evan and Ryan spent a total of $210, how much did
   Sean spend?
   a. $30
   b. $90
   c. $120
   d. $180
   e. $210

   3. _____

4. In a class , 1/3 of the students are juniors and 2/5 are seniors. The
   remaining 8 are sophomores. How many students are in the class?
   a. 12
   b. 15
   c. 18
   d. 21
   e. 30

   4. _____

5. A bag contains only red, blue and yellow marbles. The probability of     5. _____
   randomly selecting a red marble is ¼, the probability of selecting a blue one
  is 1/6. Which of the following could be the total number of marbles in the bag?
     a. 10
     b. 12
     c. 18
     d. 20
     e. 30

*__Solutions for this section can be found on page 143__*

# Various SAT Strategies

These are miscellaneous multiple choice problems. Give yourself six minutes and see how well you do.

1. If the pattern shown below were continued, what would be the sum of the first 129 numbers?

    1. _____

    $$1, 2, 4, -3, -2, 1, 2, 4, -3, -2, 1, 2, 4, -3, -2, \ldots$$

    a. -54
    b. 0
    c. 54
    d. 108
    e. 162

2. If $x = \dfrac{y}{2}$, then $2y - \dfrac{x}{2} =$

    2. _____

    a. 5y
    b. 4y
    c. 2y
    d. $\dfrac{5}{4}y$
    e. $\dfrac{7}{4}y$

Grid Ins

3. When a number k is divided by 5 the remainder is 2, what is the remainder when 6k is divided by 5?

    3 _____

4. A solution of water and alcohol is 25% alcohol. If the amount of water is doubled what percent is now alcohol?

    4. _____

5. A man cycles 3 miles north, then 6 miles west. He then goes 9 miles north and 1 mile east. How far from his starting place is he?

    5. _____

6. If x is 3/4 of y and y is 2/5 of z, what is the ratio of x to z?

    6. _____

## *Solutions to these questions can be found on page 143*

# Arithmetic Warm Up

Students in high school probably haven't studied arithmetic in a while. Most students would have a hard time defining odd, even, or prime numbers. Try these questions and be sure to study all the facts and vocabulary on the following pages.

## Easy

1. What is the greatest common factor of 32 and 28?                1. _____
   - a. 1
   - b. 2
   - c. 3
   - d. 4
   - e. 7

## Medium

2. If x is a positive integer greater than 1, and $x(x+4)$ is odd, then x must be:    2. _____
   - a. even
   - b. odd
   - c. prime
   - d. a factor of 8
   - e. divisible by 8

## Hard

3. The units digit of $2^{35}$ is how much more than the hundredths digit of    3. _____
   $\frac{.567}{1000}$?
   - a. 1
   - b. 2
   - c. 3
   - d. 4
   - e. 5

# Arithmetic Warm Up Solutions

## Easy

**1. d**

     Common factors are numbers that divide evenly into the given numbers. The greatest common factor (GCF) is the largest number that divides evenly into both of the given numbers. The find the GCF, first find the prime factorization of each of the numbers.

$$32 = 2^5 \qquad\qquad 28 = (2^2)(7)$$

The GCF is the product of the factors common to both numbers. Since they both have 2's use the lower of the exponents. Therefore, the GCF is $2^2$ or 4.

     The TI 84 and TI 83 calculators will find the greatest common factors of any two numbers. If you go into the *Math* menu and then the *Num* submenu. Option #9 is *gcd.* This represents the greatest common divisor of the given numbers. Simply type *gcd(32,28)* and the calculator will give you the greatest common divisor.

## Medium

**2. b**

     If the product of two integers is odd, then both of the numbers must have been odd. Therefore, x must be odd.

## Hard

**3. b**

     Since $\dfrac{567}{1000}$ is equivalent to .567, the hundredths digit is 6. The units digit of $2^{33}$ is a lot tougher. You should recognize that a number raised to an exponent that large is probably a time trap so you need to find a faster way (assuming your calculator can't do it). **Look for patterns within the problem.**

$$2^1 = 2$$
$$2^2 = 4$$
$$2^3 = 8$$
$$\underline{2^4 = 16}$$
$$2^5 = 3\mathbf{2}$$
$$2^6 = 6\mathbf{4}$$

You can see that after the 4th term in the pattern, the units digits begin to repeat. To find the units digit of the 35th term, divide 35 by 4. The remainder will indicate which number in the pattern the to use. When 35 is divided by 4 remainder is 3. Therefore, the units digit is 8, the 3rd number in the sequence.

     Since 8 is 2 more than 6, your answer is **b**.

# Math Vocabulary List

These are words that show up on the SAT that you will need to know.

Consecutive: Numbers in order

Respectively: the examples are in the order they are given

Difference: Answer from a subtraction problem

Sum: the answer from an addition problem

Product: the answer from a multiplication problem

Quotient: the answer from a division problem

Digit:  A number from 0 to 9

Places: In a number of more that one digit, each place has a value of more     than one.  For example there is the digit in the tens, hundreds,  thousands,…. places.

Distinct:  Different; no repetition

Even:  an integer divisible by 2

Odd: an integer NOT divisible by 2

Prime: A number divisible by only one and itself (one is NOT a prime number)

Factor: A number that divides evenly into another number.

Multiple: a larger (or equal) number that a factor goes into. For example, 12
        is a multiple of 6 and 6 is a factor of 12.

Numerator: The top of a fraction

Denominator: The bottom of a fraction

Remainder:  The number left over in a division problems.  NOT the quotient.

# Arithmetic Facts

Over the last few years it is likely that you have studied very little arithmetic. Therefore it is necessary for you to review these facts.

1. Any number is either positive, negative, or zero

2. The only number that is equal to its opposite is 0.

3. The product and quotient of two positive or two negative numbers is positive. The product and quotient of positive number and a negative number is negative.

4. The product of an even number of negative factors is positive. The product of an odd number of negative factors is negative.

5. The reciprocal of any non-zero number x is 1/x.

6. The product of any number and its reciprocal is 1.

7. A prime number is a number that is divisible only by one and itself. **The number 2 is major trap when dealing with prime numbers.** It is the smallest prime number and the only even prime number. Be aware of this if a question calls for plugging in a number!

8. Odd/Even Numbers
   Only integers can be even or odd.
   Zero is considered an even number.
   The sum or difference of 2 even or odd numbers is always even.
   If one integer is even and the other is odd, their sum and difference is odd.
   The product of two integers is even unless both of them are odd.

| Adding and Subtracting | Multiplying |
| --- | --- |
| Even+Even=Even | (Even)(Even)=Even |
| Odd+Odd=Even | (Odd)(Odd)=Odd |
| Even+Odd=Odd | (Even)(Odd)=Even |

**There is no consistent rule for division!** This is because only integers are considered even or odd. Dividing two integers will not always get you another integer.

9.  Inequalities:

If a<b, then a+c<c+b.

If a<b and c<d, then a+c<b+d.

If a<b and c is negative, then ac>bc.

If a<b and they both have the same sign, then $\dfrac{1}{a} > \dfrac{1}{b}$

10.  Watch out for F.O.N.Z. traps!!

F.  Fractions

O.  One

N.  Negative

Z.  Zero

These traps are especially important to watch out for.  When we refer to **Fractions** we are talking about the values of x in the interval 0<x<1.  The reason these are such traps is that they often do the opposite of what you expect.  For example, given that 0<x<1, look at each of the following inequalities.

$x^2 < x^1$        (the higher the exponent the lower the number)

$x < (1/x)$        (Dividing by x makes the quotient bigger)

$5x < 5$        (multiplying by x makes it smaller)

**One** is a trap because you will get the same answer whether you multiply or divide.  Furthermore, one to any exponent is always one.

You must be aware of the multiplying and dividing properties of **Negative** numbers.  You also have to be aware of exponents

$(negative)^{odd} = negative$

$(negative)^{even} = positive$

Anything multiplied by **Zero** is zero.  Therefore if xy=0, either x=0 or y=0.

# SAT Number Facts and Arithmetic Practice

Basic Questions

1. Which of the following are prime numbers? (there are more than one)     1. _____

   $1$     $\sqrt{3}$     $\dfrac{5}{4}$     $-3$     $2$     $3$     $5$     $7$     $9$

2. What is the smallest prime number?     2. _____

3. Which of the following numbers are odd? (there's more than one)     3. _____
   $0$     $1$     $-3$     $5.3$     $5/3$     $48/16$     $\sqrt{7}$

4. What is the remainder when 43 is divided by 6?     4. _____

5. What is the units digit of $2^{12}$?     5. _____

SAT Questions

6. If x is an odd number, which of the following MUST be even?     6. _____

   a. $\dfrac{x+1}{2}$

   b. $\dfrac{x-1}{2}$

   c. $x^2$

   d. $x^2 + x$

   e. $x^2 + 2x$

7. Which of the following will always be a multiple of n(n+1), if n is a positive     7. _____
   integer less than 3?
   - a. 12
   - b. 14
   - c. 15
   - d. 16
   - e. 20

8. If m is a multiple of 7 and n is a factor of 3, which of the following     8. _____
   could be equal to 17?
   - a. mn
   - b. m+n
   - c. m/n
   - d. n/m
   - e. m-n

9. If the greatest prime factor of 32 is *a* and the least prime factor of 77 is *b*, then *ab* is divisible by which of the following numbers?

    a. 3
    b. 4
    c. 5
    d. 7
    e. 9

9. _____

10. If r, s, and t are integers, rs=t and t>0 then which of the following must be true?

              I.  r<t
              II.  $s \leq t$
              III.  s>0

    a. I only
    b. II only
    c. III only
    d. I and III only
    e. II and III only

10. _____

11. Points A, B and C are on a number line. If point B is 3 units from A and C is 8 units from A, how far is C from B?

    a. 2
    b. 5
    c. 11
    d. 24
    e. Cannot be determined

11. _____

12. Which is NOT equal to 1/5 of an integer?

    a. 2/5
    b. 1
    c. 5/3
    d. 21/3
    e. 10

12. _____

13. At a deli one day the first person served was #21 and the last person served was #94. How many people were served that day?

    a. 72
    b. 73
    c. 74
    d. 115
    e. Cannot be determined

13. _____

14-15 refer to the number line shown below.

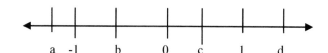

14. Which of the following MUST be true?

I. $c^2 > c^3$
II. $a^2 > c$
III. $b < (1/b)$

a. II only
b. I and II
c. I and III
d. I, II and III
e. None

14. _____

15. Which of the following statements MUST be true?

I. $ad < b$
II. $ab > ad$
III. $(1/a) > (1/b)$

a. II only
b. I and II
c. II and III
d. I, II and III
e. None

15. _____

Grid Ins

16. If $p^2 = 25$ and $q^2 = 36$, what is the largest possible value of $p-q$?

16. _____

17. The product of 2 positive odd integers is 21. What is the smallest possible value of one of the integers?

17. _____

18. The operation A# represents the sum of all the integers from A to 1 For example 5#=5+4+3+2+1=15. What is the value of 15#-13#?

18. _____

***Answers for this section can be found on page 143***

# Even and Odd Number Practice

To answer any problems that involve even and odd numbers, you must be aware of the even and odd rules.

1. If x is an odd number, which of the following MUST be even?    1. _____

$a. \dfrac{x+1}{2}$

$b. \dfrac{x-1}{2}$

$c. \; x^2 + 2$

$d. \; x^2 + x$

$e. \; 2x + 1$

2. How many elements of the set $\{0, -2, 3, 2.4, 5/3, 48/3\}$ are even?    2. _____

    a. 1

    b. 2

    c. 3

    d. 4

    e. 5

3. If x, y and z are positive integers such that the value of x-y is even    3. _____
and the value of $(x-y)^2 + x + z$ is odd, which of the following MUST be true?

    a. x is odd

    b. x is even

    c. If z is odd, then x is odd

    d. If z is odd, then xy is even

    e. z is always odd

4. J and K are both positive integers and j-k=4j-2  Which of the    4. _____
MUST be true?

                I.   J is even

                II.  K is even

               III.  J+K is even

    a. I only

    b. II only

    c. III only

    d. I and II

    e. I, II and III

5. If x and y are odd integers, which of the following must also be an odd integer?

      I. $(x+3)y$
     II. $(x+3)+y$
    III. $(x-3)-y$

   a. I only
   b. II only
   c. III only
   d. I and II
   e. II and III

5. _____

*__Answers for this section can be found on page 144__*

# Fractions, Decimals and Ratios Warm Up

Working with fractions and decimals is an important arithmetic skill that will show up often on the test. Do the warm up questions. Then study the facts in this section. When doing questions be aware of the word "ratio". This will change the meaning of the fraction in the problem.

## Easy

1. The ratio of juniors to seniors on a team is 3:5. What percentage of the team is juniors?

1. _____

## Medium

2. In the repeating decimal .3456734567...., what is the 527th digit after the decimal?

2. _____

## Hard

3. Bill did 1/5 of his homework problems during study hall. He did 5/8 of the remaining problems at home. Of the questions remaining, he could not do ¼ of them. What is the ratio of homework questions he did not know how to do to the homework questions he did know how to do?

3. _____

# Fraction/Decimal Warm Up Solutions

## Easy
### 1. **37.5**

What makes this problem a little tricky is that you are given a ratio and asked to change that to a percent. Remember, a ratio compares a part to a part while a percent compares a part to it's whole. So if the ratio is 3:5 then the percent would be $\dfrac{3}{3+5}\times100\%$

## Medium
### 2. **4**

Questions like this are very common. You can see from the decimal that there is a pattern of 5 repeated digits. Use this to your advantage. When 527 is divided by 5 the remainder is 2. This means the last digit will be the 2nd number in the pattern.

## Hard
### 3. **3/37**

These questions are easier than they look. Find a common multiple of all the denominators. In this case, 40 is the lowest. From here divide up 40 according to each situation

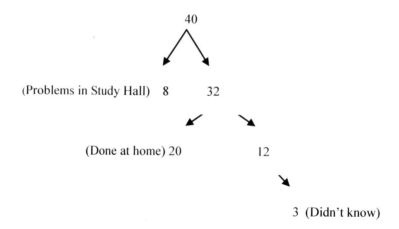

Since he didn't know how to do 3 of them, there were 37 that he did know how to do. Therefore, the ratio is 3/37.

# Fractions, Decimals, Ratios and Proportions Facts

1.  To compare two fractions , simply use your calculator and compare the decimals. In some situations, you can save time by not having to use your calculator. Here are two examples of time savers.

a.  If  you have two fractions, $\dfrac{a}{b}$ and $\dfrac{a}{c}$ and b<c, then $\dfrac{a}{b} > \dfrac{a}{c}$

b. If  you have two fractions $\dfrac{b}{a}$ and $\dfrac{c}{a}$ and b>c, then $\dfrac{b}{a} > \dfrac{c}{a}$

2. When doing operations with fractions, <u>use your calculator</u> as much as possible.

3. To multiply any decimal or whole number by 10 or a power of 10, just move the decimal as many places to the right as there are zero's.

4. To divide any decimal or whole number by 10 or a power of 10, just move the decimal as many places to the left as there are zero's.

5. When you multiply fractions, just multiply across. $\dfrac{2}{3} \times \dfrac{4}{7} = \dfrac{2 \times 4}{3 \times 7} = \dfrac{8}{21}$

6. Dividing fractions, multiply by the reciprocal of the fraction. $\dfrac{1}{5} \div \dfrac{1}{2} = \dfrac{1}{5} \times \dfrac{2}{1} = \dfrac{2}{5}$

7. Dividing by a number between 0 and 1 makes the number bigger.

8. Multiplying by a number between 0 and 1 makes the number smaller

9. A ratio represents a comparison of two parts.  A fraction represents a part of a whole..  Ratios will often be expressed in fractional form.  **Make sure you are sure whether the number shown represents a comparison of a part to a part (ratio) or a part to a whole (fraction)**

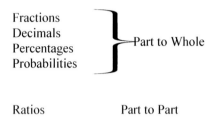

Fractions
Decimals
Percentages
Probabilities
} Part to Whole

Ratios                        Part to Part

10. If a set of objects is divided into two groups in the ratio of x:y, then the first group has

$\frac{x}{x+y}$ of the objects and the second has $\frac{y}{x+y}$ of the objects.

11. If two numbers are in a ratio of x:y then the sum of those numbers must be a multiple of x+y.

12. A proportion is a comparison of ratios.  To find a missing number in a proportion, cross multiply and solve.

# SAT Fraction and Ratio Practice (Parts and Wholes)

Basic

Solve each of the following proportions.

1. $\dfrac{x}{5} = \dfrac{6}{10}$     1. _____

2. $\dfrac{x+3}{13} = \dfrac{5x-1}{39}$     2. _____

3. A boy who is 6 feet tall casts an 8 foot shadow. How tall is a tree that casts a 36 foot shadow?

    3. _____

SAT Questions

4. If 2/3 of the people on a team are right handed, what is the ratio of left handed people on the team to right handed people on the team?

    4. _____

      a. 2:5
      b. 1:2
      c. 2:1
      d. 2:3
      e. 3:2

5. The ratio of Juniors to Seniors on a committee is 3:5. What percent of the committee is Juniors?

    5. _____

      a. 37.5%
      b. 40%
      c. 60%
      d. 62.5%
      e. Cannot be determined

6. If 75% of the applicants to a program are rejected, what is the ratio of the number of accepted to the number rejected?

    6. _____

      a. 1/4
      b. 1/3
      c. 2/3
      d. 3/4
      e. 3/1

7. The ratio of boys to girls on the track team is 3:5. Which of the following could NOT be the number of people on the team?

    7. _____

      a. 30
      b. 32
      c. 40
      d. 48
      e. 56

8  If a:b=2:5 and a:c=5:7, what is the value of b:c?          8. _____
     a.  2:7
     b.  17:10
     c.  14:25
     d.  25:14
     e.  7:2

9. After working on a new roof for X hours on Saturday, Mr. Gross          9. _____
    finished the job by working on Sunday.  In total, he spent Y hours on the
    job.  What part of the job was done on Sunday?

    $a.\ \dfrac{y}{x+y}$

    $b.\ y-x$

    $c.\ \dfrac{y-x}{y}$

    $d.\ \dfrac{y-x}{x}$

    $e.\ \dfrac{y-x}{y+x}$

Grid Ins

10.  A French class has 15 boys and 20 girls.  What part of the class          10. _____
    are boys?

11.  Tim can read 84 pages in one hour.  How many  pages can he read          11. _____
    in 40 minutes?

12.  I drove 168 miles in 3 hours and 30 minutes. At this rate, how many          12. _____
    hours will it take to drive 1272miles?

13. The ratio of the number of freshmen to sophomores to juniors to seniors on a college football team is 3:7:6:9. What percent of the team are sophomores?

13. _____

14. If 3a=4b and 3b=5c, what is the ratio of a to c?

14. _____

15. Presently, in a jar, there are 20 red ball, 40 green balls and 10 white balls. How many white balls must be added so that the probability of selecting a white ball is 2/3?

15. _____

**_Solutions for this section are on page 144_**

35

# SAT Fraction Questions

## Basic

1. $\dfrac{4}{3} + \dfrac{3}{7} =$ _____

2. $\dfrac{1}{2} \times \dfrac{2}{4} \times \dfrac{4}{8} \times \dfrac{8}{16} =$ _____

3. $\dfrac{3}{7} \div \dfrac{9}{35} =$ _____

4. $\dfrac{x+6}{x^2 - 36} =$ _____

5. *Simplify* : $\dfrac{\dfrac{1}{a} + \dfrac{1}{b}}{\dfrac{1}{a} - \dfrac{1}{b}} =$ _____

6. $1\dfrac{3}{4} \times 12 \div 7\dfrac{3}{4} =$ _____

## SAT Questions

7. If 1/x=3/5, what is the value of x?           7. _____
   - a. -3/5
   - b. 5/3
   - c. -5/3
   - d. 3/5
   - e. 15

8. If a+b=0 and a does not equal b, what is the value of a/b?           8. _____
   - a. -1
   - b. 0
   - c. ½
   - d. 1
   - e. Cannot be determined

9. Steve decided to give away some of his CD's. He gave 1/4           9. _____
   to Tom, and then he gave 2/5 of the remaining CD's to his brother.
   What is the ratio of CD's Steve kept to the ones he gave away?
   - a. 2/3
   - b. 3/5
   - c. 11/20
   - d. 9/11
   - e. 11/9

10. What is the value of x if $\dfrac{2}{3}+\dfrac{3}{7}+\dfrac{4}{5}=\dfrac{3}{7}+\dfrac{1}{x}+\dfrac{2}{3}$ ?

10. _____

11. If x were a number in between 0 and 1, put x, $x^2$ and $x^3$ in from low to high. *(A question could not be asked like this on the SAT but it's still good to be able to do it.)*

11. _____

12. What is the product of all the numbers in the sequence

$$\left(1+\dfrac{1}{2}\right)\left(1+\dfrac{1}{3}\right)\left(1+\dfrac{1}{4}\right)\dots\dots\left(1+\dfrac{1}{16}\right) ?$$

12. _____

## ***Solutions for this section are on page 144***

Solutions for this section are on page 144

# Tough!(But Easy) Fraction Problems

These are some common types of problems. Whether they are multiple choice or grid ins, you would do them the same way as questions # 3 on page 29.

1.  During a lab experiment in a biology class, 1/3 of the mice died on one day. The following day, 2/5 of the remaining mice died. What part of the original mice are still alive?

    1. _____

2.  You go to the mall and find a shirt that is marked ¼ off. If you have a coupon that entitles you to 1/5 off the marked price and a friend who has offered you their 1/3 off discount, what part of the final price would you pay?

    2. _____

3.  3 men and a woman go out to lunch and agree to split the bill equally. If the woman then offers to pay for half of one of the men's share and 1/4 of another's, what part of the total bill is she paying?

    3. _____

4.  At a conference, a number of people left early. At 2 PM 1/5 of the people left. At 3 PM, 1/3 of the remaining people left. At 4 PM, twice the number that left at 2 PM left, leaving 24 people still at the conference. How many people were originally at the conference?

    4. _____

5.  In a basket there are apples and oranges. There are 3 times as many apples as there are oranges and there are 4 times as many red apples as there are green apples. If a person were to randomly pick a piece of fruit from the basket, what is the probability of randomly selecting a green apple?

    5. _____

## *Solutions for this section are on page 145*

# Percentage Warm Up

Percents are similar to fractions in that they both represent a part of a whole. Problems often involve working with percent change and finding percents of percents. Try these questions and review the rules on page 41 before you practice.

## Easy

1. A track team has 45 members. If 9 members are freshmen, what percent of the team is NOT freshmen?

1. _____

## Medium

2. If 200% of .24 is equal to 60% of X, then X is equal to what number?

2. _____

## Hard

3. An item that usually sells for A dollars is marked down to B dollars. What is the percent of the markdown?

3. _____

$$a. \left( \frac{A+B}{B} \right) 100$$

$$b. \left( \frac{B-A}{B} \right) 100$$

$$c. \left( \frac{A-B}{A} \right) 100$$

$$d. \left( \frac{A-B}{B} \right) 100$$

$$e. (A-B)100$$

# Percentage Warm Up Solutions

## Easy

### 1. **80**

Remember that a percentage is a part of a whole. Since there are 9 freshmen, there are 36 non-freshmen. 36/45=80%.

## Medium

### 2. **.8 or 4/5**

This problem can be solved using 2 different proportions. Remember that a percent of a number can be found using the proportion: is/of=%/100. First, find 200% of .24.

$$\frac{.24}{x} = \frac{200}{100}$$

From this we are left with .48 is 60% of a number X. Doing the same proportion we get that x=.8

## Hard

### 3. **c**

Percent change is the amount of the change over the original value. If you went from A to B the change would be (A-B) and the original price was A.

# Percent Facts

Percentages are another way to represent fractions. Remember that percentages represent parts of a whole. These are basic facts involving percents that will come up.

1. A percentage represents a part of a whole. The easiest way to solve percentage problems is to set up the proportion:

$$\frac{is(part)}{of(whole)} = \frac{\%}{100}$$

2. For any positive numbers x and y, x% of y =y% of x. For example, 30% of 40 is equal to 40% of 30. This is a big time trap!

3. The percent change of a value = (amount of change)/(original amount)  The percent change going from 20 to 25 can be found by

$$\frac{25-20}{20} = .25 = 25\%$$

4. If x<y, the percent increase in going from x to y is <u>always</u> greater than the decrease going from y to x. For example, the percent change going from 40 to 50 is 25% while the percent change going from 50 to 40 is 20%.

5. If you were to start with a number and then increase it and decrease it by the same percentage (or vice versa), your result will always be less than the number you started with. For example, if you were to start with 20 and increase by 20% it would raise your number to 22. Then decreasing by 20%, you would change 22 to 19.8. This will be referred to as a "Yo-Yo Trap" in later pages.

6. A percentage decrease followed by another percent decrease will always result in a decrease that is more than the sum of the two percentages. The same can be said for increases. If you were making $100/day and got two 10% raises, your salary would go from $100 to $110 and then $121. If you got a single 20% raise, you pay would only go to $120.

7. Percents over 100% can be confusing. Remember that 100% of a certain number <u>is</u> that number. Therefore, 8 increased by 200% is 8+2(8) or 24. This also means that if an amount doubles it increases by 100%.

# SAT Percentage Practice

## Basic Questions
1. What is 20% of 40?

                                                                                    1. _____

2. 16 is what percent of 60?

   2. _____

3. 12 is 25% of what number?

   3. _____

4. A number increases from 20 to 25. What is the percent change?

   4. _____

5. What is 300% of 6?

   5. _____

## SAT Questions
6. 23% of 43 is equal to 43% of what number?

   6. _____

7. A camping tent went on sale from $80 to $60. If the same discount is applied to a sleeping bag that cost $40, what will be the price of the sleeping bag?
   - a. $50
   - b. $40
   - c. $30
   - d. $10
   - e. $5

   7. _____

8. A television set is on sale for 15% off the original price. If the sale price were $340, what was the original price of the TV?
   - a. $340
   - b. $370
   - c. $400
   - d. $440
   - e. $470

   8. _____

9. If 40% of 20% of a positive number is equal to 10% of Z percent of the same number, what is the value of Z?
   - a. 10
   - b. 20
   - c. 50
   - d. 60
   - e. 80

   9. _____

10. If a music store buys its' guitars for $50 and marks them up by 50%.
The profit is what percent of the selling price?

    a. 20%

    b. 25%

    c. 33 1/3%

    d. 40%

    e. Cannot be determined

10. _____

11. P is what percent of Q?

    a. 100PQ

    b. $\dfrac{100P}{Q}$

    c. $\dfrac{100Q}{P}$

    d. $\dfrac{P}{100Q}$

    e. $\dfrac{Q}{100P}$

11. _____

12. Tom is saving every month for a new car. If he decides to not save
anything in July and August, by what percent must his amount saved
increase the rest of the months in order to keep his annual saving the same?

    a. 16 2/3%

    b. 20%

    c. 25%

    d. 33 1/3%

    e. Cannot be determined

12. _____

Grid Ins

13. A sequence of number is written so that each number is 50% more
than the previous term. If the 1$^{st}$ number were 16 what is the 4$^{th}$ number?

13. _____

14. A student raises his average from 60 to 66. Another student, whose
average is 90 wants to increase his average by the same percentage. What will
his average increase to?

14. _____

**_Solutions for this section are on page 145_**

# Arithmetic Review

1.  If 0<x<1, which of the following is always greater than x?
    a.  $x^2$
    b.  1-x
    c.  1/x
    d.  x-1
    e.  x/(1+x)

1.  _____

2.  If x and y are prime numbers, which of the following MUST be even
    a.  xy
    b.  x+y
    c.  2x+y
    d.  x/y
    e.  2(x+y)

2.  _____

3.  The ratio of boys to girls on the track team is 2:3.  What percent
    of the team is boys?
    a.  33.3%
    b.  40%
    c.  60%
    d.  66.6%
    e.  Cannot be determined

3.  _____

4.  Which of the following represents x increased by 150% of x?
    a.  .15x
    b.  1.5x
    c.  2.5x
    d.  15x
    e.  25x

4.  _____

5.  What is the greatest of 4 consecutive integers whose sum is 82?
    a.  19
    b.  20
    c.  21
    d.  22
    e.  23

5.  _____

6. The price of a pair of shoes is d dollars. If there is a 10% off sale
   but sales tax is 10%, what will be the final price of the shoes?

      a. .81d
      b. .9d
      c. .99d
      d. d
      e. 1.09d

6 _____

7. If 3a=4b and 5b=6c, what is the ratio of a to c?

      a. 1:2
      b. 5:8
      c. 2:5
      d. 2:1
      e. 8:5

7. _____

8. If the pattern shown below were continued, what would be the sum of the
   first 137 numbers?

   $$1, 2, 4, -3, -2, 1, 2, 4, -3, -2, \ldots\ldots$$

      a. −57
      b. 0
      c. 57
      d. 108
      e. 162

8. _____

9. If 2/5 of 2/3 ÷5/6 were divided by 3/10, the result would be:

      a. 1/15
      b. 16/25
      c. 8/15
      d. 16/15
      e. 125/27

9. _____

10. When m is subtracted from 2n, the result is t. Which of the following
    expresses the result when 3m is added to n ?

       a. 5n-t
       b. 5n+t
       c. −n+t
       d. 7n-t
       e. 7n-3t

10. _____

11. Which of the following has the least number of distinct prime factors?

       a. 6
       b. 8
       c. 10
       d. 15
       e. 24

11. _____

12. 30% of 40 is 25% of what number?

12. _____

13. If a+b=3 and c-d=6, what is the value of ac-bd+bc-ad?

13. _____

14. A school club is made up of only juniors and seniors.  One third of the club members are seniors and 1/4 of the seniors are boys.  If 3/5 of the entire club are boys, what part of the club membership is junior girls?

14. _____

15. What is the value of (1+1/2)(1+1/3)(1+1/4)....(1+1/9)?

15. _____

**_Solutions for this section are on page 145_**

# Equations and Inequalities Warm Up

Working with equations and inequalities is an important skill that you will have to master. The skills discussed and practiced in this section will occur throughout the SAT in many different areas. Remember that if a question is multiple choice, use the choices!

## Easy

1.  If $4x+3=8$, what is the value of $12x+9$?                          1. _____

## Medium

2.  One solution to the equation $x^2+3x+k=0$ is 4. What is the value of k?          2. _____
    a.  -28
    b.  -12
    c.  -7
    d.  -3
    e.  4

## Hard

3.  Throughout the season the Jets scored more than 10 but less than 34 point          3. _____
    every game. Which inequality represents this range?
    a.  $|x-14|<34$
    b.  $|x-34|<10$
    c.  $|x+22|<12$
    d.  $|x-22|<12$
    e.  $|x-12|<22$

# Equations and Inequalities Warm Up Solutions

### Easy
1. **24**

       While you could solve for x fairly easily, there is an easier way.  You have to realize that the expression 12x+9 is significant because it is 3 times 4x+3.  Since,

$$4x+3=8 \qquad \textit{Multiply both sides by 3}$$
$$3(4x+3)=3(8)$$
$$12x+9=24$$

       The lesson here is that when asked to find the value of an expression, very often you should solve for the expression NOT the variable.

### Medium
2. **a**

       A root to an equation is a solution for x.  To find the value of k, simply substitute the known root in for x and solve for k.

$$x^2+3x+k=0$$
$$(4)^2+3(4)+k=0$$
$$28+k=0$$
$$k=-28$$

### Hard
3. **d**

       Absolute value represents a distance.  The format for an absolute value inequality is:

$$|x\text{-middle}|<\text{distance from the middle to the ends}$$

The middle of 10 and 34 is 22.  The minus sign in the absolute value means you will take the opposite of whatever the sign of the middle number is.  It won't always be minus.
Since the middle is 22 and the distance of 10 and 34 from the middle is 12, the inequality is:

# Equations and Inequalities Facts

1. Be aware of questions that ask you for the value of an expression. In these cases you will often solve for the expression and not necessarily the variable.

2. When solving an inequality you will switch the direction of the inequality when you multiply or divide by a negative number.

   ex. $-2x > 8$

   $-1/2(-2x > 8)$

   $x < -4$

3. Solve quadratic equations by factoring. They need to be put into standard form ($ax^2 + bx + c$) and set equal to zero.

$$x^2 + 4x - 12 = 0$$
$$(x+6)(x-2) = 0$$

   $x + 6 = 0 \qquad\qquad x - 2 = 0$

   $x = -6 \qquad\qquad\quad x = 2$

4. The sum of the roots of a quadratic equation is $-b/a$. The product of the roots is $c/a$.

5. When solving an absolute value equation, isolate the absolute value and break the equation into the positive case and negative cases. Solve each one individually.

   $|x+3| - 4 = 7$      *Add 4 to both sides*

   $|x+3| = 11$      *Break into positive and negative cases*

   $x + 3 = 11 \qquad x + 3 = -11$      *Solve each*

   $x = 8 \qquad\qquad x = -14$

6. A radical equation is solved by isolating the radical and then squaring both sides.

   $\sqrt{x+3} - 4 = 2$      *Add 4 to both sides*

   $\sqrt{x+3} = 6$      *Square both sides to get rid of radicals*

   $x + 3 = 36$

   $x = 33$

7. If a quadratic equation can't be factored, you have to use the quadratic formula. Once the equation is in the form $ax^2 + bx + c = 0$, the solution would be

$$x = \frac{-b \pm \sqrt{b^2 - 4ac}}{2a}$$

8. If a quadratic equation is graphed it will form a parabola. If the coefficient of the $x^2$ is positive, the parabola will open upward (smiley faced), if it is negative it will open downward (frown faced).

9. The discriminant is the part of the quadratic formula that is inside the radical. The discriminant will tell you the nature of the roots and how the parabola formed by the equation will intersect the x axis.

| Discriminant | Nature of the Roots | Graph |
|---|---|---|
| $b^2-4ac<0$ | imaginary | Completely above or below the x axis |
| $b^2-4ac=0$ | Real, rational, equal | The graph will be tangent to the x axis |
| $b^2-4ac>0$ and a perfect square | Real, rational, unequal | The graph will touch the x axis at two points where the x values are rational |
| $b^2-4ac>0$ and not a perfect square | Real, irrational, unequal | The graph will touch the x axis at two points where the x values are irrational |

# SAT Equations and Inequalities Practice

<u>Basic</u>

1. Solve for x:  2x+6=4x-6        1. _____

2. Solve for x:  |x+4|-3=5        2. _____

3. Solve for x:  $x^2+3x-10=0$       3. _____

$$\sqrt{x+2}-3=5$$

4. Solve for x:            4. _____

5. Solve for x:  2(x-3)<3-x        5. _____

<u>SAT Questions</u>

6. At what point(s) will the graph of $y=x^2+2x-24$ touch the x axis?   6. _____
    a. x= -24 and x= 2
    b. x= -2 and x=24
    c. x=6 and x=-4
    d. x= -6 and x=4
    e. x=12 and x=-2

7. If $4^{x+2}=2^{x-1}$, what is the value of x?      7. _____
    a. -5
    b. -2
    c. -1
    d. 1
    e. 4

8. The solutions to the equation $x^2+8x+k=0$ are equal to each other. What is   8. _____
    the value of k?
    a. -16
    b. -8
    c. -4
    d. 8
    e. 16

9. The function $x\Delta y$ represents $x(x+y)$. If $x\Delta 4 = 21$ what could be the value of x?

    a. -10
    b. -7
    c. -3
    d. 10
    e. 21

9. _____

10. If $(x-6)(x-k)=x^2-3kx+m$. What is the value of k?

    a. -6
    b. -3
    c. 3
    d. 6
    e. Cannot be determined

10. _____

11. Which number is NOT be in the solution set of $x^2+x\geq 2$?

    a. -3
    b. -2
    c. -1
    d. 1
    e. 3

11. _____

12. Solve for x: $\sqrt{x+1}+\sqrt{x-4} = 5$

    a. 3
    b. 4
    c. 5
    d. 7
    e. 8

12. _____

13. If John can finish a job in 4 hours and James can finish the same job in 6 hours. How long would it take them to finish the job together?

    a. 1.6 hours
    b. 2.4 hours
    c. 3.5 hours
    d. 5 hours
    e. 10 hours

13. _____

14. The temperature during the winter in Antarctica ranges from -60 to -10. Which inequality represents this range?

    a. $|x+10|<60$
    b. $|x-10|<-60$
    c. $|x-35|<25$
    d. $|x+35|<25$
    e. $|x+35|<-25$

14. _____

**_Solutions for this section are on page 146_**

# Exponents Warm Up

You probably first learned rules of exponents in middle school. Exponents are an important topic in your regular math class and they show up often on the SAT. Be sure to familiarize yourself with all the rules involving exponents and radicals on the following pages.

## Easy

1. If $(3x)^2 = 81$ then x=

    a. 2
    b. 3
    c. 6
    d. 9
    e. 12

1. _____

## Medium

2. If a>0, b<0, and c<1, assuming c does not equal 0, which of the following must be true?

    a. abc is positive
    b. abc is negative
    c. $a^2b^2c$ is positive
    d. $ab^4c^2$ is positive
    e. $ab^3c^5$ is negative

2. _____

## Hard

3. The value of $3^x + 3^x + 3^x$ is:

    a. $9^x$
    b. $3^{3x}$
    c. $9^{3x}$
    d. $3^{x+3}$
    e. $3^{x+1}$

3. _____

# Exponents Warm Up Solutions

## Easy

**1. b**

Since $(3x)^2=81$, $3x$ must be either 9 or -9. Since none of the choices are negative, $x=3$.

## Medium

**2. d**

This is a FONZ question. (If you forgot what FONZ stands for, see page 23) Any number raised to an even exponent will be positive. Since you don't know the value of c (it could be positive or negative), you need both b and c to be raised to an even exponent in order to guarantee your answer is positive.

## Hard

**3. e**

Know your exponent rules. It'd be really easy to combine them and say $9^x$ or $3^{3x}$. However, there is no exponent rule for the addition of terms. Turn this into a multiplication problem:

$$3^x+3^x+3^x \qquad \textit{Combine like terms}$$
$$3(3^x) \qquad \textit{When you multiply, add the exponents}$$
$$3^{x+1}$$

Another option is to pick a number for x and plug it in. If x=1, the you would have $3^1+3^1+3^1=9$. Plugging 1 into the choices eliminates all of them except choice a and e. Just pick a different number and test it into choices a and e.

# Exponent and Root Rules

There are several rules you need to know concerning exponents and roots for the SAT. Some rules you learned a couple of years ago, some are relatively new.

## Exponent Rules

I. $(x^5)(x^4)=x^9$ — When you multiply terms with the same base, add exponents

II. $(x^5)^4=x^{20}$ — Power of a power, multiply exponents

III. $\dfrac{x^7}{x^2}=x^5$ — When you divide terms with the same base, subtract exponents

IV. $x^1=x$ — Anything to the first power is itself

V. $x^0=1$ — Anything the zero power is one

VI. $x^{-1}=\dfrac{1}{x^1}$ — Negative Exponent=Flip!

VII. $x^{\frac{a}{b}}=\sqrt[b]{x}^{a}$ — A fractional exponent creates a root.

VIII. $(xy)^a=x^a y^a$ — This one can be sneaky! If the exponents of two numbers are the same, you can multiply the numbers. Keep the exponents the same.

## Radical Rules

I. $\sqrt{x}\sqrt{y}=\sqrt{xy}$ — You CAN multiply radicals of different numbers.

II. $\sqrt{x}+\sqrt{y}\neq\sqrt{x+y}$ — Common mistake! You can't break up the radical when the expressions inside are being added or subtracted from each other.

III. $\sqrt{x^2}=x$ — The resulting exponent is exponent divided by the index

III. $\sqrt{x^2+y^2}\neq x+y$ — Another common mistake!

# SAT Exponents and Roots Practice

Basic
Perform each operation and express your answer in simplest form.

1. $x^2y - 9x^2y$ _____

2. $(5x^2y^4)^2$ _____

3. $(3)^{3x}(5)^{3x}$ _____

4. $15^{x+3} \div 15^{x-1}$ _____

5. $2^3 * 2^4$ _____

6. $\left(a\sqrt{4}\right)\left(a\sqrt{4}\right)$ _____

7. $\sqrt{8} + \sqrt{18}$ _____

8. $\dfrac{12\sqrt{30}}{3\sqrt{6}}$ _____

SAT Questions

9. Which is the following is equal to $2^{6x}$?                           9. _____
                   I.   $(2^{3x})^2$
                   II.   $(4^{3x})$
                   III.   $(2^{3x})(2^{2x})$
   a. I
   b. II
   c. III
   d. I and II
   e. II and III

10. $(7^7)(7^7)$ could also be expressed as:                           10. _____
                    I.   $7^{14}$
                    II.   $49^7$
                    III.   $49^{14}$

    a. I
    b. II
    c. III
    d. I and II
    e. II and III

11. If $9\sqrt{x} - 7\sqrt{x} - 36 = -16$, then x=                           11. _____
    a. 5
    b. 10
    c. 20
    d. 50
    e. 100

12. If $8=a^x$, then $64a$ is equivalent to: 12. _____

    a. $a^{2x+1}$

    b. $a^{4x+1}$

    c. $a^{8x}$

    d. $a^{4x}$

    e. $a^{8x+1}$

13. If $2^x=3$, what is the value of $2^{x+2}$? 13. _____

    a. 3

    b. 6

    c. 9

    d. 12

    e. 27

Grid Ins

14. If $(x^m)(x^3)=x^{14}$ and $(x^3)^n=x^{12}$, what is the value of m+n? 14. _____

15. $9^3 * 27^2 = 3^n$. What is the value of n? 15. _____

16. If $2^x=5$, what is the value of $4^{x-1}$? 16. _____

**_Solutions for this section are on page 147_**

# Polynomial Warm Up

As you take higher levels of math in high school and beyond, you will see more complex problems dealing with polynomials and factoring. Luckily, the SAT will not get too complicated. You should be comfortable with factoring as well as all operations with polynomials.

## Easy
1. If $x^2-y^2=30$ and $x+y=6$, what is the value of $x-y$?            1. _____

      a. 3        b. 4        c. 5        d. -6        e. Cannot be determined

## Medium
2. The length and width of a rectangle are $(x+6)$ and $(x+2)$ respectively. If        2. _____
   the length is decreased by 2 and the width is increased by 2, how has the
   area of the rectangle changed?
   - a. stayed the same
   - b. decreased by 4
   - c. decreased by 2
   - d. increased by 2
   - e. increased by 4

## Hard
3. If $x^2-2x-15=(x+r)(x+s)$ for all values of x, one possible value of r-s is:        3. _____
       a. 8        b. 2        c. -2        d. -3        e. -5

# Polynomial Warm Up Solutions

## Easy
**1. c**

$x^2-y^2$ factors out to $(x+y)(x-y)$. Therefore, $(x+y)(x-y)=30$. When given that $(x+y)=6$, you can substitute to get $6(x-5)=30$. Therefore, $(x-y)=5$. Remember, **solve for the expression, not the variable.**

## Medium
**2. e**

Don't bother solving for x. Multiply out your expressions:
$(x+6)(x+2)=x^2+8x+12$.
Decreasing the length by 2 and increasing the width gives you:
$(x+4)(x+4)=x^2+8x+16$
You can see that the product after the change is 4 more than the product before the change.

## Hard
**3. a**

Factoring $x^2-2x-15$ gets you $(x-5)(x+3)$. The difference of -5 and 3 is either -8 or 8 depending on the order. The only possible solution is 8.

# SAT Polynomials and Factoring Facts

1. There are 3 SAT polynomials that show up VERY frequently.
   <u>Memorize</u> these so you can save time:
   a. $(x+y)(x-y)=x^2-y^2$
   b. $(x+y)^2=(x^2+2xy+y^2)$
   c. $(x-y)^2=(x^2-2xy+y^2)$

   **Remember that $x^2+y^2$ can NEVER be factored! This is a common mistake.

2. Make sure that you read the questions fully and that you're NOT doing too much work. Remember that in certain situations you need to solve for an EXPRESSION and not necessarily the VARIABLE(S) involved.

3. In order to multiply two binomials you would multiply the first terms, then the outside terms, the inside terms and finally the last terms. Many schools use the abbreviation F.O.I.L. This stands for First Outside Inside and Last. For example, if the you were to multiply $(x+3)$ and $(x+2)$ you would get $x^2+2x+3x+6$ which combines to $x^2+5x+6$.

4. The roots of an equation represent the values of x where the equation is equal to zero. Graphically, they represent the x coordinate of the point where the graph hits the x axis.

5. Given an equation of the form $y=ax^2+bx+c$, the sum of the roots is $-b/a$ and the product of the roots is $c/a$.

6. When adding or subtracting remember to only combine like terms. Like terms are terms with the same variables and the same exponents.

# SAT Polynomials and Factoring Practice

## Basic
Factor each of the following.

1. $x^2-36$ _____

2. $100-w^2$ _____

3. $x^2+8x+16$ _____

4. $x^4-81$ _____

Express each of the following products in simplest terms.

5. $(x+3)^2$ _____

6. $(x+y)(x-y)$ _____

7. $(4-x)(4+x)$ _____

8. $\left(x+\sqrt{5}\right)^2$ _____

## SAT Questions

9. If x>0 and x=3y, then $\sqrt{x^2+2xy+y^2}$ =

    a. 4y
    b. 5y
    c. 20y
    d. 25y
    e. 30y

9. _____

10. If $kx^2+y=ky^2+x$, what is the value of k in terms of x and y?

    $a.\ x+y$
    $b.\ x-y$
    $c.\ xy$
    $d.\ \dfrac{1}{x+y}$
    $e.\ \dfrac{1}{x-y}$

10. _____

## Grid Ins
11. The value of $x^2-y^2=24$. If the (x+y) is 8, what is the value of (x-y)?

11. _____

12. $$\frac{a^2 - b^2}{a + b} = 8$$ , where a+b does not equal 0.  What is the value of a-b?       12. _____

13. If $(x+y)^2=36$ and $x^2+y^2=20$, what is the value of xy?       13. _____

14. The product of (3x+2) and $(x^2+5x-3)$ is the polynomial $Ax^3+bx^2+cx+d$.  What is the value of c?       14. _____

15. How much bigger is the area of a square whose sides are (x+4) than the area of a rectangle whose length is (x+6) and width is (x+2)?       15. _____

16. If $x^2+y^2-16=9-2xy$, what is the value of (x+y)?       16. _____

17. If $x^2+x=12$, what is the value of $3x^2+3x-6$?       17. _____

**_Solutions for this section are on page 147_**

# Systems of Equations Warm Up

Solving systems of equations in your math class can usually be a little difficult algebraically. Doing them on the SAT can be pretty simple if you do them the right way. Give these questions a try and review the facts on the following pages.

## Medium

1. If a+b=6, b+c=-3 and a+c=5, what is the value of a+b+c?        1. _____

## Hard

2. If 6x+4y=7 and x-y=2, what is the value of 2x+2y?        2. _____

# System of Equations Warm-Up Solutions

## Medium

1. **4**

   Adding all three equations gives you the equation:
   $$2a+2b+2c=8$$
   From this, we can solve that $a+b+c=4$.

## Hard

2. **2**

   If adding the equations doesn't work, try to subtract them. In this case;

   $$\begin{array}{r} 6x+4y=7 \\ -\,(x-\ y=2) \\ \hline 5x+5y=5 \end{array}$$

   Since $5x+5y=5$, then $x+y=1$. Therefore, $2x+2y=2$

# Systems of Equations

When you have two linear equations, the solution represents the point at which both lines will intersect.

A system of equations can have one solution (one intersection), no solutions (the two lines are parallel) or infinite solutions (the two lines overlap).

There are several ways to solve a system of equations. One of the most basic is by simply graphing the two equations using your calculator and finding the intersection.

The second way is through substitution. In this method you would solve one equation for one variable and then substitute that solution into the other equations.

Ex) $3x+2y=13$
$x+y=7$          *Solve for y (y=7-x), then substitute this into the first equation*

$3x+2(7-x)=13$  *Now solve the equation for x. When you have your solution, substitute that in to one of the equations to solve for y.*

The third way is through addition. Using this method, you will multiply one or both of the equations by a constant so that when the equations are added, one of the variables will cancel out.

Ex)     $3x+2y=13$      *If the first equation were multiplied by 3*
        $2x+3y=12$      *and the second by -2 you would get:*

        $9x+6y=39$
        $\underline{-4x-6y=-24}$    *Adding these, you would get*
        $\dfrac{5x}{5}$    $\dfrac{=15}{5}$

        $X=3$           *Now you can substitute this value to solve for y.*

Often on the SAT you will see different types of equations where you will be asked to solve for an expression, not a variable. When this happens the first course of action should be to add the two equations. If this doesn't happen, then subtract them.

**Solve for the expression, NOT the variables.** Both of the warm up questions were examples of this.

# SAT Systems of Equations Practice

<u>Basic:</u>
Use any method to solve the systems of equations.

1. $4x+3y=5$      1. _____        2. $3x-4y=2$      2. _____
     $2x+4y=0$                                      $x+y=10$

3. At a baseball game, the price of a 3 sodas and 2 hotdogs is \$13.      3. _____
   The price of 1 soda and 4 hotdogs is \$16.  What is the price of a hotdog?

<u>SAT Questions</u>

4. If r=$\sqrt{x^2+2xy+y^2}$ $and$ $s=\sqrt{x^2-2xy+y^2}$ , what is r-s?      4. _____
   a. $2x$
   b. $2y$
   c. $x+y$
   d. $x^2+y^2$
   e. $x^2-y^2$

<u>Grid Ins</u>
5. If the value of $3x+4y$ is 11 and the value of $2x+2y$ is -2, what is the      5. _____
   value of $5x+6y$?

6. If $5x+4y=10$ and $3x-4y=-2$, what is the value of $2x+8y$?      6. _____

7. If 4x+2y=8 and x+3y=7, what is the value of 3x+3y?

7. _____

8. If 4x+2y=12 and 3y=-6x+k have an infinite set of solutions, what is the value of k?

8. _____

9. Three different color marbles are in a bag. The weight of the blue and red marbles is 12 ounces. The red and green ones weigh 14 ounces and the blue and green ones weigh 8 ounces. If the weight of each is a whole number, how many ounces is the green marble?

9. _____

**_Solutions for this section are on page 148_**

# Averages Warm Up

Questions on averages can be great because whether they show up as easy, medium or hard questions you would do them in very similar ways. For questions involving rates remember that **Distance=(Rate)(Time).** Give the warm ups a try then review the facts.

## Easy

1. The average of 4 numbers is 10. When a $5^{th}$ number is added, the average increases to14. What number was added?

1. _____

## Medium

2. The average of 6 different numbers is 6. If 2 were subtracted from 4 of the numbers, what would the new average be?

2. _____

## Hard

3. You drive 30 miles per hour for the first 50 miles of a trip, then 50 miles per hour for the remaining 3 hours. What is your average speed?

3. _____

# Averages Warm Up Solutions

## Easy
### 1. 30

Find the total. If 4 numbers have an average of 10, then they must have added to 40. If 5 numbers have an average of 14, then the total is 70. The difference is 30

## Medium
### 2. 4.66 or 14/3

Work with the total. If 6 numbers have an average of 6 then they must add to 36. By taking 2 away from 4 of the numbers, you are reducing the total by 8. If 6 numbers add up to 28, their average is 4.66

## Hard
### 3. 42.8 or 42.9

Using the formula that distance=(rate)(time) you can solve that your rate=(dist)/(time)

$$\text{Rate} = \frac{50 + 150}{1\frac{2}{3} + 3}$$

Simplifying this we get an average rate of 42.86 mph.

# Facts on Averages

1. The diagram below is very useful for questions comparing averages. We'll refer to them as "Before-After" questions. The number of scores times the average will give you the total number of whatever is being compared. The total divided by either of the bottom numbers will give you the other bottom number. (VERY IMPORTANT!)

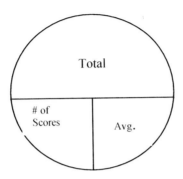

2. If all the numbers in a group are the same, then that number is the average of the group.

3. The total deviation above the mean is the same as the total deviation below the mean.

4. If the average of a set of numbers is X and a number, N, is added to the set, then the average will go up, down, or stay the same, depending on whether N is above, below or equal to N.

5. If a set has an odd number of consecutive elements, the average will be the middle term. If a set has an even number of consecutive elements, the average of the set will be the average of the two middle terms.

6. Rate questions can be tricky. To find the average rate be sure to look at the TOTAL distance divided by the TOTAL time.

7. The median represents the middle number when all the numbers are placed in order. If there is an even number of numbers, the median will be the average of the middle two numbers.

# SAT Averages Practice

## Basic

1. Express the average of x, 3x+4 and 2x+8 in terms of x.

1. _____

2. The mean of 4, 7, 8, 11 and x is 10.  What is the value of x?

2. _____

3. From the table below, find the average score.

3. _____

| Score | Freq. |
|-------|-------|
| 2 | 1 |
| 4 | 1 |
| 6 | 4 |
| 8 | 3 |

4. Using the same table, find the median score.

4. _____

## SAT Questions

5. The average of two numbers is A. If one of the numbers is B, what is value of the other number in terms of A and B?

5. _____

        a. $A - B$

        b. $B - A$

        c. $2A - B$

        d. $B - 2A$

        e. $\dfrac{A + B}{2}$

6.. What is the average of $2^{10}$ and $2^{20}$?

6. _____

        a. $2^{15}$

        b. $2^{30}$

        c. $2^{29}$

        d. $2^5 + 2^{10}$

        e. $2^9 + 2^{19}$

7. If a 30% percent salt solution were combined with a 50% salt solution, which could be the concentration of the resulting mixture?

                              I. 40%
                              II. 49%
                              III. 50%

    a. I only
    b. II only
    c. I and II only
    d. II and III only
    e. I, II, and III

7. _____

Grid Ins

8. If your average after 4 tests is an 80, what do you need on your 5<sup>th</sup> test to raise your average to an 82?

8. _____

9. Your average after 4 tests is an 80. What is the lowest you can grade you can receive on your 5<sup>th</sup> test and still finish with a 85 average after 7 tests (the highest possible score on a test is 100)?

9.

10. The average of 6 different integers is 15.  If the average of the highest
    and the lowest numbers is 20, what the average of the remaining 4 integers?

10 _____

11. The average of 5 different positive integers is 98.  If the 1$^{st}$ two
    integers are 58 and 76 and the rest are over 100, what is the largest
    possible value of one of the remaining integers?

11. _____

12. In a class of N students the average on a test was 82.  On the same
    test, a class of P students had an average of 94.  If the average of both
    classes together was 90, what is the ratio of P to N?

12. _____

13. If you drove 70 miles per hour for one hour of a 3 hour trip, how fast
    would you have to drive (in miles per hour) the remaining 2 hours to
    average 60 miles per hour for the entire trip?

13. _____

*__Solutions for this section are on page 149__*

# Functions Warm Up

Functions are one of the most important topics in upper level mathematics. Luckily, most of the really advanced concepts are not on the test. For the SAT you will have to know basic notation, evaluating functions algebraically and graphically, and how to shift functions.

## Easy

1. If $f(x)=x^2+3x-2$, what is the value of $f(3)$?

1. _____

## Medium

2. If the graph of $f(x)=(x+4)^2-2$ were shifted two units to the left and 4 units up, what would be the resulting equation?

        a. $f(x)=(x+2)^2+4$
        b. $f(x)=(x+2)^2+2$
        c. $f(x)=(x+2)^2-6$
        d. $f(x)=(x+6)^2+2$
        e. $f(x)=(x+6)^2-2$

2. _____

## Hard

3. At time $t=0$, a ball was thrown upward from an initial height of 6 feet. Until the ball hit the ground, its height , in feet, after t seconds was given by the function:

$$h(t)=c-(d-4t)^2$$

where c and d are both positive constants. If the ball reached a maximum height of 108 feet at a time of $t=2.5$ seconds, what is the height of the ball at $t=2$?

3. _____

# Functions Warm Up Solutions

## Easy
### 1. 16

When evaluating f(x), the number x inside the parenthesis is the input. Plug 3 into the equation so that

$$f(3)=(3)^2+3(3)-2=16$$

## Medium
### 2. d

A function in the form f(x+h)+k has been shifted –h units horizontally and k units vertically. It's important to note that the horizontal shift is always in the opposite direction of the sign. Therefore, the initial function $f(x)=(x+4)^2-2$ has been shifted 4 units to the left and 2 units down from the origin. By moving it 2 more units to the left and 4 units up it becomes $f(x)=(x+6)^2+4$

## Hard
### 3. 104

The function will be an upside parabola since it the equation that contains the $x^2$ is negated. The vertex of the parabola $y= -x^2$ passes through the point (0,0). Since the maximum of h(t) is 108, the value of c must be 108. By substituting this and the coordinates of the maximum into the equation we get

$$(108)=(108)-(d-4(2.5))^2$$

solving for d gives us d=10. Therefore the function for the height of the ball after t seconds is $h(t)=108-(10-4t)^2$. Using this h(2)=104.

# Function Facts

1. A function can be written several different ways. Y=, f(x)=, g(x), ..... They all represents the same things. To go from f(x) to g(x) in the same problem represents two different functions.

2. The number that goes into the function, x, is an element of the domain. The number that comes out of the function is an element of the range.

3. Know the general shapes and form of basic functions. You should know what linear, quadratic and absolute value functions looks like.

4. If the x and y switch places then the graph of the function will be reflected in the line y=x. The graph of $x=y^2$ is still a parabola, but it is sideways.

5. When you are evaluating a composition of functions, the x(input) will go through the composition from right to left.

   Ex. Given the functions f(x)=4x+3 and g(x)=x$^2$

   $$g \circ f(3) = $$
   
   f(3)=4(3)+3=15
   g(15)=(15)$^2$=<u>225</u>

6. To evaluate a function from a graph, trace from the x axis to the function and then from the function to the y axis.

7. Graphs of functions can be moved. If you start with the function f(x), then the function f(x-h)+k represents the function f(x) after a horizontal shift of h units and a vertical shift of k units. It is VERY important to remember that the horizontal shift will always go in the opposite direction of the sign.

8. Inverse variation is when x and y multiply to a constant.

   Ex. xy=constant

9. Direct variation is when the ratio of x and y is a constant.

   $$Ex. \frac{x}{y} = Constant$$

# SAT Functions Questions

Basic
1. Given the function $f(x)=4x+3$, evaluate $f(3)$.

1. _____

2. Given the function $f(x)=x^2+x$, for what value(s) is $f(x)=6$?

2. _____

3. What is the domain of the function $f(x)= \sqrt{3x+6}$ ?

3. _____

4. If the domain of the function $f(x)=4x-2$ were restricted to $-3 \leq x \leq 3$, what would be the corresponding range?

4. _____

SAT Questions
5. For which function is $f(-2)=f(2)$?

5. _____

    a. $f(x)=4x^3$
    b. $f(x)=x/5$
    c. $f(x)=3x-1$
    d. $f(x)=x^3-4$
    e. $f(x)=5+|x|$

6. The domain of $f(x)=x^2+2$ is $-3 \leq x \leq 3$. What is the difference between the largest and the smallest elements of the range?

6. _____

    a. 0
    b. 7
    c. 9
    d. 11
    e. 18

7. If $f(x)=3x-9$ and $g(x)=\dfrac{x}{3}+2$ then $f(g(x))=$

7. _____

    a. x-7
    b. x-3
    c. x-1
    d. 9x-1
    e. (x/3)+2

8. The graph of the function $f(x)=(x+2)^2-4$ is shifted 3 units down
and 2 units to the left. What is the equation of the new graph?

    a. $f(x)=(x-2)^2-7$
    b. $f(x)=(x+4)^2+1$
    c. $f(x)=(x+4)^2-7$
    d. $f(x)=(x-0)^2+1$
    e. $f(x)=(x-0)^2-7$

8. _____

Answer 9-11 using the graph below

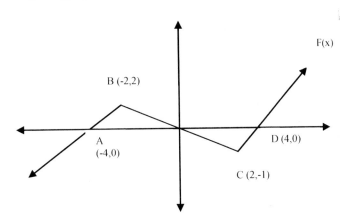

9. What is the value of $f(f(-2))$

    a. -4
    b. -2
    c. -1
    d. 2
    e. 4

9. _____

10. In what interval(s) is $f(x)<0$?

    a. $x<-4$
    b. $x<0$
    c. $(x<0)$ and $(0<x<4)$
    d. $(x<-4)$ or $(0<x<4)$
    e. $(x>4)$ or $(-4<x<0)$

10. _____

11. If $g(x)$ is defined as $f(x+2)-2$, what is the $g(-4)$?

    a. -7
    b. -2
    c. 0
    d. 1
    e. 2

11. _____

12. What is the domain of the function $f(x) = \dfrac{4}{\sqrt{x-4}}$ ?

    a. $x > 4$

    b. $x \geq 4$

    c. $x < 4$

    d. $x \leq 4$

    e. Cannot be determined

12. _____

## Grid Ins

13. If the operation $a\#b$ is defined as $\dfrac{a+b}{a-b}$ , for what value of b is $5\#b=3$?

13. _____

14. Given the function $g(x) = x^2 - 3x + k$, if $g(5) = 13$. What is $g(2)$?

14. _____

15. The values of x and y vary inversely. If $x=6$ when $y=6$, what is the value of y when $x=4$?

15. _____

16. The function $f(x)$ is defined as $f(x) = x^2 - 2x$. If $f(x) < 8$, what is one possible positive integral value of x?

16. _____

**_Solutions for this section are on page 149_**

# Sequence Warm Ups

While number patterns have always been on the exam, arithmetic and geometric sequences are also now included. Very often questions involving sequences are time traps. You may get them right, but if you do them the wrong way you will use up way more time than you should.

Easy
1. What is the 12$^{th}$ term of the sequence 3, 7, 11, .....?           1. _____

Medium
2. A lighthouse blinks every 8 seconds while a nearby signal           2. _____
   beacon blinks every 12 seconds. Over the course of ten minutes,
   how many times will they blink at the same time?

Hard
3. In the geometric sequence shown below,           3. _____
                   a, b, c, d, e, f, g, ....
   each term after the first term is r times the previous term.
   For example, (r)(a)=b, (r)(b)=c and so on. If (g/a)=729, what is the value
   of (e/c)?

# <u>Sequence Warm Up Solutions</u>

## <u>Easy</u>
### 1. 47

It's an arithmetic sequence since 4 is being added. To find the twelfth term use the formula $a_n=a_1+d(n-1)$. Substituting in the appropriate values we get:

$$a_{12}=3+4(12-1)=47$$

## <u>Medium</u>
### 2. 25

10 minutes is equal to 600 seconds. With the first light blinking every 8 seconds and the 2nd every 12 seconds, that means they blink together ever 24 seconds. 600 divided by 24 is 25. So, over the course of 10 minutes they will blink together 25 times.

## <u>Hard</u>
### 3. 9

In a geometric sequence you multiply by a fixed multiple (r) to get each successive term. Because of this $b=a(r)$, $c=a(r)^2$ ..... The sequence could be rewritten as a, ar, $ar^2$, $ar^3$, $ar^4$, $ar^5$, .... The ratio $\dfrac{g}{a}=\dfrac{ar^6}{a}=r^6$. Since $r^6=729$, r=3. Therefore, $\dfrac{e}{c}=\dfrac{ar^4}{ar^2}=r^2=9$

# Sequence Facts

A sequence is just a pattern of numbers. On the SAT you will see 3 different kinds of sequences. The most common can be found by finding the pattern within the sequence. For example:

What is the $53^{rd}$ term of the sequence: 2,4,6,8,2,4,6,8,2,4,6,8…..

Since only 4 terms in the sequence are repeated over and over, just divide the 53 by 4. Since the remainder is 1, the $53^{rd}$ term is the $1^{st}$ term of the sequence.

The other types are a little more complicated. They are arithmetic and geometric sequences.

<u>Arithmetic:</u>  a sequence where there is a common difference between each successive term. To find the $n^{th}$ term of a sequence use the formula

$$a_n=a_1+d(n-1),\ \text{where}$$
$a_n$= the $n^{th}$ term of the sequence
$a_1$= the first term of the sequence
d=the common difference
n=the term you are looking for

<u>Geometric:</u>  a sequence where there is a common ratio between successive terms. To find the $n^{th}$ term of a geometric sequence you would use the formula:

$$a_n=a_1(r)^{n-1}$$ , where r is the common ratio of consecutive terms (multiple). The way to find the value of r is to divide one term by the term before it.

*The formulas for arithmetic and geometric sequences are NOT given to you! Be sure to memorize them.*

# Sequence Problems

1. The first term of the sequence of numbers shown below is 4. Each even-numbered term is 2 more than the previous term and each odd numbered term, after the first, is -1 times the previous term. For example, the second term is 4+2 and the third term is (6)(-1). What is the 55$^{th}$ term of the sequence?

4, 6, -6, .....

    a. 4
    b. 6
    c. 2
    d. -4
    e. -6

1. _____

Grid Ins

2. Using the sequence from the previous question, what is the sum of the first 11 terms of the sequence?

2. _____

3. What is the 43$^{rd}$ term of the sequence 4,5,6,7,4,5,6,7......?

3. _____

4. What is the 85$^{th}$ term of the sequence 2,5,8, 11.....?

4. _____

5. What is the absolute value of the 49$^{th}$ term of the sequence 9,6,3, 0.....?

5. _____

6. A carpenter is making a railing out of 4 different kinds of wood. He plans on using 6 inch sections of oak, maple, ash and cherry in that order throughout the length of the 13 foot rail. How many *feet* of oak will he use?

6. _____

7. If the first term of an arithmetic sequence is 7 and the $12^{th}$ term is 51, what is the $15^{th}$ term?

7. _____

8. What is the units digit of $2^{100}$?

8. _____

9. A ball dropped from a ladder bounces 16 feet on its first bounce. Each successive bounce will be 75% the height of the previous bounce. How high is the $4^{th}$ bounce?

9.

***Answers for this section can be found on page 150***

# Algebra Review

Algebra is an important subject on the SAT. At this stage in your high school career, you should be pretty solid on the basics. As you saw in the polynomial section, there are still ways that the writers of the SAT like to present questions that can make them more challenging. The purpose of this section is to expose you to some of the algebra problems you might encounter on the SAT.

1. What is the average of $2^8$ and $2^{12}$?

    a. $2^{10}$
    b. $2^4 + 2^6$
    c. $2^{19}$
    d. $2^{18}$
    e. $2^7 + 2^{11}$

1.

2. If $\dfrac{x}{y} = \dfrac{s}{t} - 1$, *then* $\dfrac{t}{s} =$

    *a.* $\dfrac{y}{x+y}$

    *b.* $\dfrac{x}{xy+x}$

    *c.* $(x+y)^2$

    *d.* $\dfrac{1}{x}$

    *e.* $\dfrac{1}{x+1}$

2.

3. The lightest person on a wrestling team weighs 96 pounds and the heaviest weighs 210 pounds. Which inequality expresses this relationship?

    *a.* $|x - 210| < 96$

    *b.* $|x + 57| < 153$

    *c.* $|x - 153| < 57$

    *d.* $|x - 57| < 153$

    *e.* $|x - 153| > 57$

3.

4. Given the equation $(x+4)(x-4) = x(x+p)$, what is the value of p?

    a. 16
    b. -216
    c. -16/x
    d. 16/x
    e. (16-x)

4.

5. Given the equation $(x+y)=(x-y)^{-1}$, if $x=3$, then $y=$

    *a.* $\pm 2$

    *b.* $\pm 8$

    *c.* $\pm 2\sqrt{2}$

    *d.* $\pm 1$

    *e.* $0$

                       5. _____

6. Given that $x<y<z$ and the average of x, y, and z is equal to three times their median, the average of x and z is how many times the average of x, y and z?

    a. ½

    b. 4/3

    c. 2

    d. 4

    e. 8

                       6. _____

Grid Ins

7. Given the equation: $3/7+2/5-4/9=1/x-4/9+2/5$, what is the value of x?

                       7. _____

8. If the operation # is defined by $m\#=m^2-1$ and the operation * is defined by $n*=n-1$, for what positive value of x is $(x*)\# = 15$?

                       8. _____

9. If $(ax+b)^2=4x^2+12x+c$, what is the value of b+c?

                       9. _____

10. If $(rx+t)^2=9x^2+px+25$, what is the value of p?

                       10. _____

11. Given the equation $4x+12=2(y+3)+6$, what is the value of x/y?

                       11. _____

12. At a football game, the ratio of freshmen to sophomores is 2:3. The ratio of sophomores to juniors is 5:6. What is the ratio of freshmen to juniors?

12. _____

13. The average of a, b, c and d is equal to 6 and the average of a and b is 10. What is the value of c+d?

13. _____

14. The average of s, t, v and w is 12 and the average of s and t is 8. If v is 4 more than w, what is the value of w?

14. _____

15. If $x^2-y^2=36$ and $x^2+2xy+y^2=81$ what is the value of $x^2-2xy+y^2$?

15. _____

16. If $4x+3y=12$ and $x+2y=18$, what is the value of $2x+2y$?

16. _____

## Solutions to this section are on page 151

Solutions to this section are on page 151

# Lines and Angles Warm Up

The topic of lines and angles is important because it is the foundation of all areas of geometry. Be sure to know your facts involving straight and parallel lines.

## Easy

1. Two supplementary angles are in a ratio of 4:5. What is the measure of the smaller angle?

1. _____

## Medium

2. In the figure below, lines L and M are parallel. What is the value of x?

2. _____

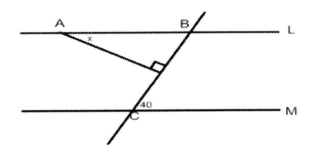

     a. 25
     b. 30
     c. 35
     d. 40
     e. 50

## Hard

3. In the figure below, lines L, M and N are parallel to each other. What is the measure of VQR?

3. _____

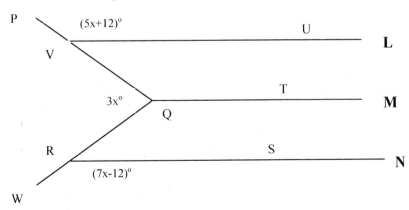

# Lines and Angles Warm Up Solutions

**Easy**
**1. 80**

      Supplementary angles add up to $180^o$. Using their ratio, $4x+5x=180$. Solving, we get $x=20$. The smaller angle was represented by $4x$. The smaller of the two angles is $80^o$

**Medium**
**2. 50**

      If lines L and M are parallel, angle ABC is the alternate interior angle with the $40^o$ angle making the measure of ABC $40^0$. Since the angles of a triangle add up to $180^o$, $x=50$.

**Hard**
**3. 72**

      Lines L and M are parallel to each other. Angle PVU corresponds with angle VQT. Since corresponding angles are congruent, $m<VQT=(5x+12)$. Lines M and N are parallel to each other. Angle WRS corresponds with angle RQT. Therefore, $m<RQT=(7x-12)$. This gives you three angles around point Q with measures of $3x$, $5x+12$ and $7x-12$. The angles around a point add up to $360^o$. Solving the equation: $3x+5x+12+7x-12=360$ gives us $x=24$. Therefore angle VQR has a measure of $72^o$.

# Line and Angle Facts

1. Know the different types of angles:
   Acute: less than 90 degrees
   Right: equal to 90 degrees
   Obtuse: between 90 and 180 degrees
   Reflexive: More than 180 degrees.
   Supplementary: 2 angles that add to 180 degrees
   Complementary: 2 angles that add to 90 degrees

2. A straight line has 180 degrees

3. When given points on a line, NEVER assume the order is the same as is given in the problem unless the problem says so.

4. A rotation around a point contains 360 degrees

5. A line that bisects an angle will cut the angle in half.

6. When two lines intersect they create vertical angles. Vertical angles are congruent. Adjacent angles are supplementary.

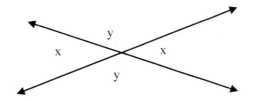

7. When two parallel lines are cut by a transversal, the following types of congruent angles are formed.

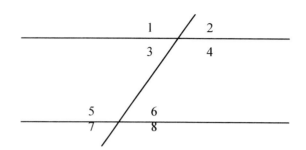

| Corresponding | Vertical | Alternate Interior | Alt. Exterior |
|---|---|---|---|
| (1,5)  (2,6) | (1,4) (2,3) | (3,6)  (4,5) | (1,8) (2,7) |
| (3,7)  (4,8) | (5,8) (6,7) | | |

In this situations, any pair of angles that are not congruent to each other are supplementary to each other.

# <u>Line and Angle Problems</u>

## Basic
Solve for x in each of the following problems.

1.

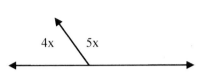

2.

1. _____

2. _____

3.

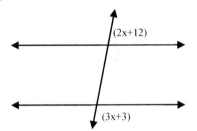

4.

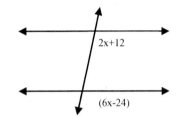

3. _____

4. _____

5. Two complementary angles are in a 2:7 ratio.  What is the measure of the smaller angle?

5. _____

6. In the diagram below, segment PA bisects angle BAC.  If the measure of angle BAC is 84°, what is the value of x?

6. _____

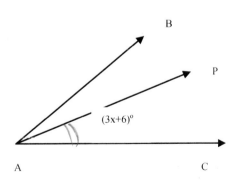

## SAT Questions

7. The measure of the supplement of an angle is 50 more than twice the measure of the complement of the angle. Which of the following equations can be used to find the measure of the angle?

   a. 90-x=(180-x)+50
   b. 180-x=2(90-x)+50
   c. 180-x=2(x-90)+50
   d. 180-x=2(50+x)
   e. 180-x=2x+50

8. On a line containing points A, B and C, point B is 4 units from A and C is 6 units from B. What is the length of AC?

   a. 2
   b. 4
   c. 6
   d. 10
   e. Cannot be determined

9. In the figure below, m<ABE=125° and m<CBD=135°. What is the m<DBE?

   9. _____

   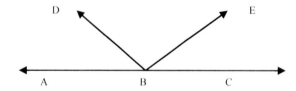

   a. 40
   b. 50
   c. 65
   d. 70
   e. 80

10. In the figure below, lines L and M are parallel to each other. If a=50 and b=120, what is the value of c?

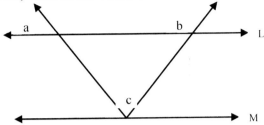

    a. 40
    b. 50
    c. 60
    d. 70
    e. 80

11. In the figure below, what is the value of x if lines L and M are parallel?

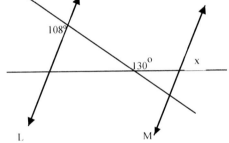

    a. 36
    b. 46
    c. 58
    d. 61
    e. 72

12. In the figure below, what is the value of x+y?

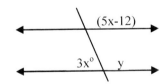

    a. 105
    b. 112
    c. 132
    d. 140
    e. 155

13. In the figure below, m is parallel to n and l bisects <ABC. The measure of angle DBC is between 45 and 55 degrees. What is one possible value of x?

13. _____

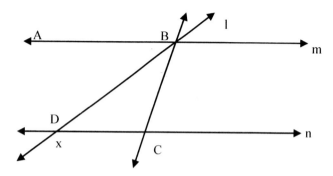

Picture not drawn to scale.

14. Points A, B, C, and D are on line L in that order. AD=40, AB=1.5BC, and BC=.4 CD. What is the length of AC?

14. _____

15. In the figure below, lines AC and BD are parallel. What is the value of x?

15. _____

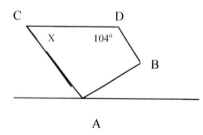

16. In the figure below, what is the value of x+y?

16. _____

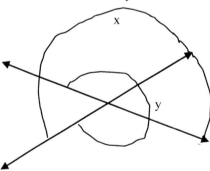

**_Answers for this section can be found on page 152_**

# Triangle Warm Up

The legend of the Trojan Horse tells the story of how Greek soldiers hid inside a giant wooden horse to conquer the city of Troy. The SAT will hide triangles inside other shapes in a very similar way. It is very important to understand all of the rules involving triangles so that you don't get caught by these "Trojan Horse" questions.

## Easy

1. What is the average of x and y in the picture below?                    1. _____

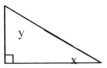

## Medium

2. In the picture below, AB=BC=6 and CD=2. Find the length of AD.          2. _____

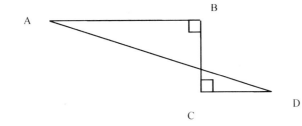

Picture not drawn to scale

## Hard

3. In the diagram below, the lengths of AB, AE and DE are equal and the    3. _____
   measures of angles ABC and CDE are 30°. If AB=5, what is the perimeter
   of ABCDE?

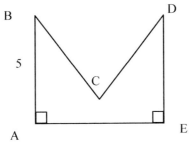

Picture is not drawn to scale

   $a.\ 15 + 10\sqrt{2}$

   $b.\ 15 + 10\sqrt{3}$

   $c.\ 25$

   $d.\ 25\sqrt{2}$

   $e.\ 25\sqrt{3}$

# Triangle Warm Up Solutions

## Easy
### 1. 45

In a right triangle, the two non-right angles always add up to 90 degrees. Their average will always be 45.

## Medium
### 2. 10

You don't want to do this as a two different triangles. Be extending the sides as shown below, you would form a single right triangle whose legs are 6 and 8. Using the Pythagorean Theorem, we get the hypotenuse to be 10.

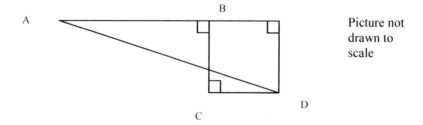

Picture not drawn to scale

## Hard
### 3. c

This a question that looks like it is a 30-60-90 triangle question. However, if you were to draw a line connecting B and D it gets a lot simpler. It would form a square with sides of 5. Since m<ABC and m<CDE=30, angles CBD and CDB will both have measures of 60 making triangle BCD equilateral. Therefore, segments BC and CD both have lengths of 5 making the perimeter of ABCDE 25.

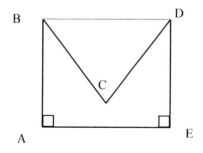

# Triangle Facts

You might think that triangles are very easy, but no fact is too small.  Triangles can be hidden in many other types of geometry problems.  These we call Trojan Horse problems because they look like one thing but they have something else inside them.  Be sure to know ALL of these triangle facts.

1.  The sum of the angles of a triangle is $180^\circ$.

2.  The smallest side is always opposite the smallest angle.  The largest side is always opposite the largest angle.

3.  Triangles are categorized by sides and by angles.  Know them all.

| Side | Angle |
|------|-------|
| Scalene-All different lengths | Acute-all angles under $90^\circ$ |
| Isosceles-Only 2 equal sides | Right-One right angle |
| Equilateral-All equal sides | Obtuse-One angle measure over $90^\circ$ |

4.  Any two sides of a triangle MUST add to more than the length of the third side.

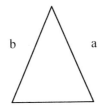

Largest integral $3^{rd}$ side:  $(a+b)-1$
Smallest integral $3^{rd}$ side:  $(a-b)+1$

5.  Any exterior angle will be equal to the sum of the two remote interior angles.
         $C=a+b$

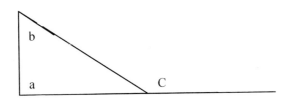

6.  Be sure to know the Pythagorean Theorem! $a^2+b^2=c^2$
    This is probably the most important triangle fact because it shows up so often in other types of problems. The legs that form the right angle are represented by $a$ and $b$ and the hypotenuse is represented by $c$.

7.  Know and memorize the **Pythagorean Triplets**. They are huge time savers
    3, 4, 5
    5, 12, 13
    7, 24, 25
    8, 15, 17
    These are sets of numbers that satisfy the Pythagorean Theorem and always are whole numbers. Not only do these numbers work, but their multiples will also work.
    For example, 3, 4, 5 multiplied by 2 is 6, 8, 10 which satisfies the Pythagorean Theorem because $6^2+8^2=10^2$.

8.  Special Right triangles (30-60-90 and the 45-45-90) are given to you but you want to know them anyway. Be aware of the clues that lead to them.

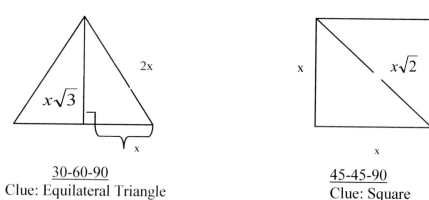

30-60-90
Clue: Equilateral Triangle

45-45-90
Clue: Square

It is also important to know that often they will give you a 45-45 right triangle where the hypotenuse is a whole number. The sides of that triangle would look like this:

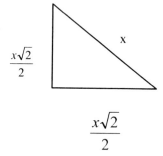

9.  The area of an equilateral triangle whose side is x is $A = \dfrac{x^2\sqrt{3}}{4}$ . You can derive it from the 30-60-90 triangle, but it is easier to know it ahead of time.

# Triangle Problems

## Basic

1. If two sides of a triangle are 13 and 7, and the third side is an integer, then the longest possible length is _____. The shortest possible length is _____.

2. The angles in a triangle are in a 2:3:4 ratio. The smallest angle is _____

3. In the picture below what is the value of x _____

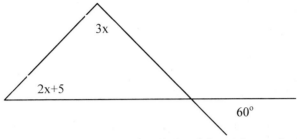

4. In each of the triangles below, find the length of the side marked x.

a. 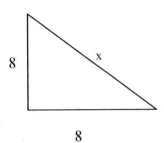    b. 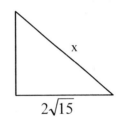    4a. _____

4b. _____

## SAT Questions

5. In triangle ABC, the lengths of the sides are 4, 5, and 7. The largest angle of triangle ABC must be:

    a. $90^o$
    b. exactly $30^o$
    c. acute
    d. obtuse
    e. Cannot be determined

5. _____

6. A square is inscribed within a circle. If the area of the square is 64, what is the area of the circle in terms of $\pi$ ?

    a. $4\pi$
    b. $8\pi$
    c. $16\pi$
    d. $32\pi$
    e. $64\pi$

6. _____

7. In the figure below, an equilateral triangle is drawn inside a square whose perimeter is 40. What is the area of the shaded region?

   *a.* 10

   *b.* 75

   *c.* $100\sqrt{3}$

   *d.* $20 - 10\sqrt{3}$

   *e.* $100 - 25\sqrt{3}$

8. In the diagram below ABC is an equilateral triangle and CD=BD. What is the distance from A to D?

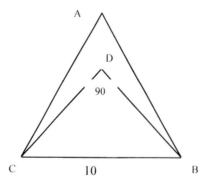

   *a.* 5

   *b.* $5\sqrt{2}$

   *c.* $5\sqrt{3}$

   *d.* $5\sqrt{3} - 5$

   *e.* $5\sqrt{3} - 5\sqrt{2}$

9. The sides of a triangle are different integral values.  What is the smallest the perimeter of the triangle could be?

9. _____

    a.  3
    b.  5
    c.  6
    d.  8
    e.  9

10.  In the diagram below AB+CD=CB,  and AD=10.  What is the length of  CB?

10. _____

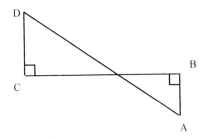

    *a.* 5

    *b.* $5\sqrt{2}$

    *c.* $5\sqrt{3}$

    *d.* 10

    *e.* $10\sqrt{2}$

11. What is the perimeter of triangle ABC?

11. _____

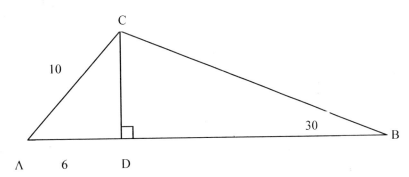

    *a.* 40

    *b.* $40\sqrt{2}$

    *c.* $40\sqrt{3}$

    *d.* $32+8\sqrt{2}$

    *e.* $32+8\sqrt{3}$

12. What is the smallest possible perimeter of a triangle with exactly two equal sides if the sides are all integral values?

     a. 3
     b. 4
     c. 5
     d. 6
     e. Cannot be determined

12. _____

## Grid Ins

13. Using the triangle shown below, what is the average of a, b, and c?

13. _____

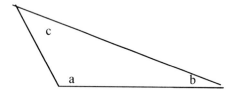

14. The sides of a triangle are consecutive odd integers. What is the the smallest the perimeter of the triangle could be?

14. _____

15. In the triangle below, what is the value of x?

15. _____

Picture not drawn to scale.

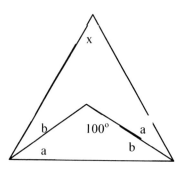

106

16. In the diagram below, what is the value of x?

16. _____

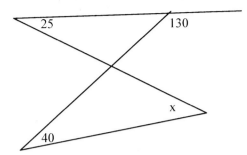

17. A man rides his bicycle 3 miles north, then 6 miles east. After a
    short break, he travels another 5miles north and 9 miles east. Exactly how
    many miles is he from his starting place?

17. _____

18. In the figure below, the ratio of the length of AD to DB is 3:5. If the area
    of ABC is 40, what is the area of triangle ACD?

18. _____

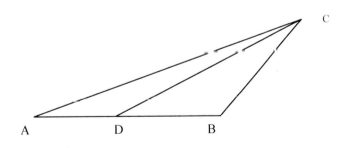

### *Answers for this section can be found on page 154*

# Coordinate Geometry Warm Up

Coordinate geometry questions involve formulas such as slope, midpoint and distance. You also have to be very aware of right triangles. If you look carefully, the distance formula is simply the Pythagorean Theorem. Like most other areas of geometry, these are common Trojan Horses.

## Easy

1. If the endpoints of the diameter of a circle are (3,2) and (-3, 10), what is the equation of the circle? (This is NOT how an SAT questions would be formatted but the topics will come up)

1. _____

## Medium

2. Triangle ABC is a right triangle. The coordinates of A and B are (1,2) and (-4, 14) respectively. If AC is parallel with the x axis, find the perimeter of triangle ABC.

2. _____

## Hard

3. In the diagram shown, the slope of line A is 1/3 and the slope of line B is -2. If the points (a,6) and (-2,b) are on lines A and B respectively what is the value of a/b?

3. _____

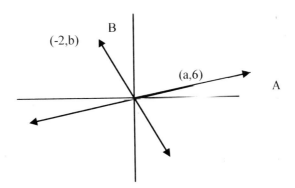

# Coordinate Geometry Warm Up Solutions

## Easy

**1.** $(x-0)^2+(y-6)^2=25$

A question in this form wouldn't be on the SAT, but it is a good question that covers several areas of coordinate geometry and is relatively straight forward. The standard form for a circle with center (h,k) and radius r is $(x-h)^2+(y-k)^2=r^2$. The midpoint of a diameter will always be the center of the circle. Using the midpoint formula we get the center to be (0,6). The length of the radius can be found using the distance formula to find the distance from the center to the either one of the endpoints of the diameter. Notice that the length of the radius can be found using a Pythagorean triplet (3,4,5). Be sure to know your Pythagorean Triplets.

## Medium

**2. 30**

Since AC is parallel to the x axis, C has to be the right angle and the coordinate of C are (-4,2). The means that the length of AC is 5 and BC is 12. Using Pythagorean Triplets (5, 12, 13) we know that AB is 13. Therefore the perimeter of triangle ABC is 30.

## Hard

**3. 9/2**

The slope of a line is defined by its rise over its run or m= $\dfrac{y_2-y_1}{x_2-x_1}$ .
Both lines go through the origin, so we have two points on each line. If the slope of A is 1/3,
then $\dfrac{1}{3}=\dfrac{6-0}{a-0}$ . Solving gives us a=18. The slope of B is -2. Therefore,
$$\dfrac{-2}{1}=\dfrac{b-0}{-2-0}$$
.
This gives us b=4. The ratio of a to b is 18/4 or 9/2.

# **Coordinate Geometry Facts**

1. Know your basic formulas!

$$\text{Slope=} \quad \frac{\Delta y}{\Delta x} = \frac{y_2 - y_1}{x_2 - x_1}$$

$$\text{Midpoint=} \quad \left( \frac{x_1 + x_2}{2}, \frac{y_1 + y_2}{2} \right)$$

$$\text{Distance=} \quad \sqrt{(x_2 - x_1)^2 + (y_2 - y_1)^2}$$

2. Be able to identify positive and negative slopes by sight.

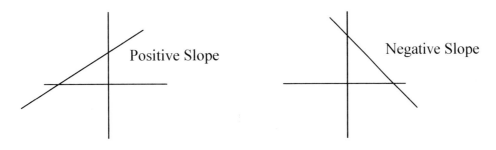

3. The slope of any line (that's not vertical or horizontal) going through the origin and another point (x,y) will always be y/x

4. The slope of a vertical line is undefined and the slope of a horizontal line is 0.

5. Be sure to know the Pythagorean triplets. They show up very often in distance problems. The most common are (3, 4, 5), (5, 12, 13), (7, 24, 25), (8, 15, 17).

6. The slopes of parallel lines are equal.

7. The slopes of perpendicular lines are negative reciprocals of each other. For example, if lines A and B are perpendicular and the slope of A is 1/3, then the slope of B is -3/1.

# SAT:  Coordinate Geometry

Answer all of the following questions.

1.  Simplify:   $4\sqrt{12}$

1. _____

2.  What is the slope of the line formed by the points (3,2) and (-1,6)?

2. _____

3.  What is the midpoint of the line segment formed by the points  A(1,-5) and B(5,7)?

3. _____

4.  What is the length of the line segment formed by the points A(1,6) and and B(4,0)?

4. _____

5.  The midpoint of AB is (4,2).  If the coordinates of A are (1,-3), what are the coordinates of B?

5. _____

## SAT Questions

6.  If point A has coordinates (3,5), point B has coordinates (3,2) and ABCD is a square, which of the following could be the coordinates of point C?
    a. (4,2)
    b. (6,2)
    c. (6,6)
    d. (4,6)
    e. (8,2)

6. _____

7.  If line A is a vertical line passing through the point (2,6) and line B is a horizontal line passing through the point (-3, -1), at what point does line A intersect line B?
    a. (6, -1)
    b. (2,-3)
    c. (2, -1)
    d. (6, -3)
    e. (-3,6)

7. _____

8. If the point (6, -8) is on a circle whose center is the origin, which of the following points are also on the circle?

    a. (0,10)
    b. (-8,6)
    c. (-6,-8)
    d. All of the points
    e. None

8. _____

9. The slope of a line containing the points (x,2) and (4,k) is -1/2. What is the value of x/k?

    a. 2
    b. 1
    c. -1
    d. ½
    e. -2

9. _____

10. The coordinates of the midpoint of segment AB are (3,4). If the coordinates of A are (-1,1), what are the coordinates of B?

    a. (4, 3)
    b. (7, -1)
    c. (7, 7)
    d. (-4, -2)
    e. (-3,-4)

10. _____

11. If the lines with equations y=x and y=x+4 are drawn on the same set of axes. What is the shortest distance between the two lines?

    a. 4
    b. $2\sqrt{2}$
    c. $4\sqrt{2}$
    d. 2
    e. $\sqrt{2}$

11. _____

12. In the diagram below, what is the perimeter of triangle ABC?    12.

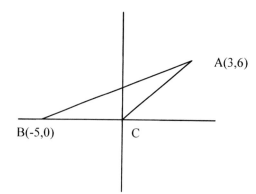

a. 15

b. 21

c. $15 + 3\sqrt{5}$

d. $15 + 5\sqrt{3}$

e. $15 + \sqrt{15}$

Grid Ins

13. In the diagram shown below points (j,k) and (m,n) which are the x and y    13.
intercepts of line A.  What is the value of k+m?

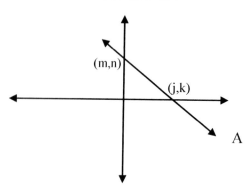

*Answers for this section can be found on page 157*

114

# Quadrilateral/Polygon Warm Up

Be sure to know all the properties of the angles and sides of quadrilaterals. You should be familiar with the differences between squares, rectangles, parallelograms and any other quadrilaterals. As before, watch out for Trojan Horses.

## Easy
1. What is the perimeter of a square whose area is 36?

1. _____

## Medium
2. The length of a rectangle is 12. If the perimeter is 42, what is the rectangle's area?

2. _____

3. The measure of an exterior angle of a regular polygon is $20°$. What is the sum of the interior angles of the polygon?

3._____

## Hard
4. The perimeter of a regular hexagon is 48  What is its area?

      *a.* $8\sqrt{3}$

      *b.* $16\sqrt{3}$

      *c.* $48\sqrt{3}$

      *d.* $64\sqrt{3}$

      *e.* $96\sqrt{3}$

4. _____

# Quadrilateral/Polygon Warm Up Solutions

## Easy

### 1. 24

The area of a square is found by the formula Area=(side)$^2$. If the area is 36, then the side has a length of 6. The perimeter of a square is found by the formula P=4(side). Using this we get a perimeter of 24.

## Medium

### 2. 108

The length and width of a rectangle will add up to half of its' perimeter. Since the perimeter is 42 and the length is 12, (12)+(width)=21. Using this, we get the width to be 9. The area is (12)(9)=108.

### 3. 2880

In any polygon, the measure of an exterior angle and an interior angle are supplements to each other. Since the exterior angle is 20°, the measure of the interior angle is 160°. The relationship between the measure of an exterior angle and the number of sides is shown be the equation 360=(n)(measure of exterior angle) where n is the number of angles. Setting up the equation 360=(n)(20) we get n=18. You will always have the same number of interior angles as you do side. Therefore, the sum of the interior angles is (18)(160) which is 2880.

## Hard

### 4. e

This isn't a hard question if you know the formula for the area of a regular hexagon. It is :

$$A = \frac{3s^2\sqrt{3}}{2}$$ .

If the perimeter is 48, then each side is 8. Plugging this into the formula give us $96\sqrt{3}$ .

# Quadrilateral/Polygon Facts

1. The opposite sides of a parallelogram are congruent and parallel.

2. Opposite angles of a parallelogram are congruent. Consecutive angles are complementary.

3. Diagonals of a parallelogram bisect each other.

4. Diagonals of rectangle are congruent.

5. Diagonals of a rhombus are perpendicular.

6. Diagonals of a square are both congruent and perpendicular to each other.

7. The sum of the angles of a quadrilateral is $360°$.

8. The diagonal of a square creates two 45-45-90 right triangles.

9. When one diagonal of a rectangle is drawn, the two triangles formed will be congruent. When both diagonals are drawn, the opposite triangles are congruent, but all 4 triangles formed will have the same area.

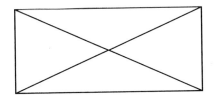

10. The sum of the interior angles of any polygon can be found with the formula **S=(n-2)180** where n is the number of sides of the polygon. To find the measure of each angle, assuming they are all equal, simply divide this number by n.

11. The sum of the exterior angles of any polygon is <u>always</u> $360°$. To find the measure of any single angle, assuming they are all equal, divide 360 by the number of sides.

12. If two polygons are similar, their sides will all be in the same ratio (r). The perimeters of the polygons will also be in this ratio. The areas, however, will be in a ratio that is the square of the ratio of the sides $(r)^2$.

For example, the ratio of the perimeters of the two squares below, is 1:3. However the ratio of their areas is 1:9.

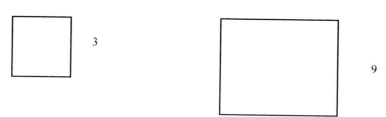

13. A regular polygon is a polygon in which every side has an equal length and the measure of every angle is equal.

14. Quadrilaterals are often "Trojan Horse" problems. Drawing a diagonal in a rectangle or square will always create two congruent (equal) right triangles. Always be watching for Pythagorean Triplets and Special Right Triangles.

# <u>Quadrilateral/Polygon Practice</u>

## Basic

1. In parallelogram ABCD, if the measure of angle A is 35°, what is the measure of angle B?

1. _____

2. The lengths of the diagonals of a rhombus are 12 and 16. What is the perimeter of the rhombus?

2. _____

3. What is the sum of the interior angles of an octagon?

3. _____

4. If a regular polygon had 12 sides, what is the measure of one of the exterior angles?

4. _____

5. The sides of a rectangle are 8 and 15. What is the length of its' diagonal?

5. _____

## <u>SAT Questions</u>

6. What is the perimeter of the figure below?

6. _____

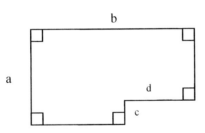

    a. 2(a+b)
    b. 2a+b+c+d
    c. a+b+2c+2d
    d. 2(a+b+c+d)
    e. (ab)

7. An equilateral triangle, a square and a regular pentagon with the same areas have sides of lengths *t*, *s*, and *p* respectively. Which of the following must be true?

7. _____

        a. t<s<p
        b. s<t<p
        c. t<p<s
        d. p<s<t
        e. s<p<t

119

8. A regular hexagon is inscribed within a circle whose area is $36\pi$. What is the area of the hexagon?

    *a.* $6\pi$

    *b.* $36\pi\sqrt{3}$

    *c.* $36\sqrt{3}$

    *d.* $54\pi\sqrt{3}$

    *e.* $54\sqrt{3}$

9. Given rectangle ABCD, E is the midpoint of AB. If the area of trapezoid DEBC is 4/5, what is the area of ABCD?

    a. ½
    b. 1
    c. 16/15
    d. 6/5
    e. 11/5

10. The length of each side of a square is increased by 50%. What is the ratio of the area of the old square to the area of the new square?

    a. 2:3
    b. 4:9
    c. 1:4
    d. 1:3
    e. 1:2

11. The diagonals of two squares are in a ratio of $1:2\sqrt{2}$. What is the ratio of their areas?

    *a.* $1:2$

    *b.* $1:2\sqrt{2}$

    *c.* $\sqrt{2}:2$

    *d.* $1:4$

    *e.* $1:8$

12. In the square shown below, the length of the diagonal is 12. What is the area of the shaded region?

12. _____

13. An exterior angle of a regular polygon has a measure of 20°. How many sides does the polygon have?

13. _____

14. In rectangle ABCD, diagonals AC and BD intersect at E. If the lengths of AB and BC are 6 and 8 respectively, what is the area of triangle ABE?

14. _____

***Answers for this section can be found on page 158***

# Circle Warm Ups

The formulas for area and circumference are given to you. Be sure to know the relationships between arcs and angles of a circle. These are also possible Trojan Horse questions.

## Easy

1. What is the area of a circle whose circumference is $10\pi$?

   a. $5\pi$
   b. $10\pi$
   c. $20\pi$
   d. $25\pi$
   e. $100\pi$

1. _____

## Medium

2. The area of the circle below is $49\pi$. If the measure of angle AOC is $60^{\circ}$ and the measure of angle OCB is $30^{\circ}$, what is the length of segment AB?

2. _____

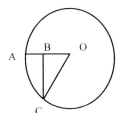

   a. 2
   b. 2.5
   c. $\dfrac{7\sqrt{3}}{2}$
   d. $7 - \dfrac{7\sqrt{3}}{2}$
   e. $\dfrac{7}{2}$

## Hard

3. In the circle shown below, OA=AB=6. What is the area of the region between chord AB and arc AB?

3. _____

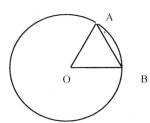

   a. $9\sqrt{3}$
   b. $6\pi$
   c. $36\pi$
   d. $36\pi - 9\sqrt{3}$
   e. $6\pi - 9\sqrt{3}$

# Circle Warm Up Solutions

## Easy

**1. d**

The formulas needed for this problem are C=πd and A=πr². From the given information we know that the diameter of the circle is 10. Therefore, the radius is 5. This means the area is 25π

## Medium

**2. e**

From the given information, we know that the radius of the circle is 7. Triangle OBC is a 30-60-90 right triangle. The ratio of the sides of a 30-60-90 triangle is

1: $1\sqrt{3}$ :2. Side OB is opposite the 30 degree angle. The length of OB=7/2. Segment OA is a radius, so AB =AO-OB. Therefore, AB=7/2.

## Hard

**3. e**

Triangle AOB is an equilateral triangle with a length of 6. Angle AOB has a measure of 60°. Therefore, the area of sector AOB is $\dfrac{60}{360}\pi 6^2$ $or$ $6\pi$ . The area of an equilateral triangle can be found with the equation A= $\dfrac{s^2\sqrt{3}}{4}$ where s=the length of the side. Therefore, the area of the shaded region is $6\pi - 9\sqrt{3}$

# Circle Facts

1. A circle is defined as the set of points equidistant from a single point.

2. A circle has 360°.

3. In a circle, all the radii are equal. This means that any triangle formed by connecting two radii MUST be isosceles.

4. The formulas for the circumference and area of a circle are:
$$C = \pi d$$
$$A = \pi r^2$$

5. A central angle is equal to its intercepted arc.

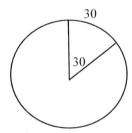

6. The measure of an inscribed angle is ½ of its intercepted arc.

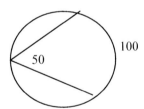

7. A tangent drawn to a circle will touch the circle in only one point. A radius touching a tangent at the point of tangency will always form a right angle with the tangent.

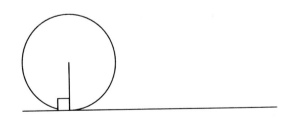

# Circle Questions

## Basic

1. What is the measure of an inscribed angle that intercepts an arc of 140°?

1. _____

2. The area of a circle is 36π. What is its' circumference?

2. _____

3. The circle shown below has a radius of 10. What is the area of the sector formed by central angle AOB whose measure is 45°?

3. _____

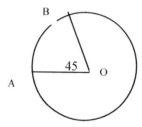

## SAT Questions

4. What is the circumference of a circle whose area is 10π?

4. _____

    a. $5\pi$

    b. $2\pi\sqrt{5}$

    c. $10\pi$

    d. $2\pi\sqrt{10}$

    e. $20\pi$

5. A square with an area of 16 is inscribed within a circle. What is the area of the circle?

5. _____

    a. $4\pi$

    b. $2\pi\sqrt{2}$

    c. $4\pi\sqrt{2}$

    d. $8\pi$

    e. $16\pi$

6. What is the length of arc ACB if the radius of circle O is 6?  6. _____

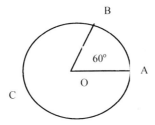

a. $1\pi$
b. $2\pi$
c. $4\pi$
d. $6\pi$
e. $10\pi$

7. If the area of a circle is doubled, what is the ratio of the old circumference  7. _____
to the new circumference?
a. $1:2$
b. $1:\sqrt{2}$
c. $1:4$
d. $1:2\sqrt{2}$
e. Cannot be determined

8. In the picture below, AB is tangent to circle O at A. If the measure of  8. _____
angle O is twice the measure of angle B and the area of circle O is $16\pi$, what
is the area of triangle ABO?

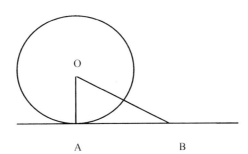

a. $4\pi$
b. $4\sqrt{3}$
c. $4\pi\sqrt{3}$
d. $8\sqrt{3}$
e. $16\sqrt{3}$

9. The 3 circles below each have an area of $9\pi$ and are tangent to each
other. What is the area of the region in the center that is not within any of
the circles?

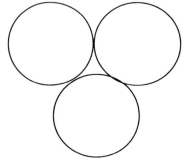

a. $9\sqrt{3}$

b. $9\sqrt{2}$

c. $9(\sqrt{3} - \pi)$

d. $9\left(\sqrt{2} - \dfrac{\pi}{2}\right)$

e. $9\left(\sqrt{3} - \dfrac{\pi}{2}\right)$

10. In the picture below two tangent circles are inside a rectangle. If the sides
of the rectangle are tangent to the circles, what is the area of the shaded region?

4
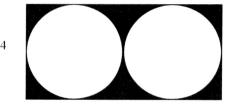

a. $8\pi$

b. $24\pi$

c. $32-4\pi$

d. $32-8\pi$

e. $32\pi$

11. In diagram below, rays AB and BC are drawn tangent to circle O at an angle of 60° to each other.  If the area of the circle is 4π, what is the area of quadrilateral OABC?

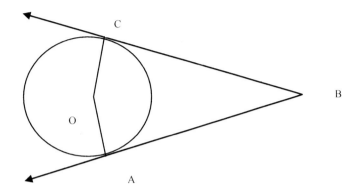

a. 4

b. 4√3

c. 8

d. 8√3

e. 8√2

Grid Ins

12.  In the circle below with center O, what is the value of x if the measure of arc AB is 80°?

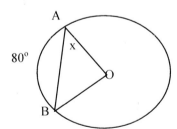

13. The area of the outer square is 196. What is the area of the inner square?

13. _____

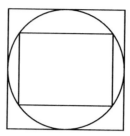

Diagram is not drawn to scale.

14. A square is inscribed within a circle. If the area of the circle is $16\pi$, what is the area of the square?

14. _____

15. If O is the center of the circle below and the length of CO and AB equal, what is m<BOC?

15. _____

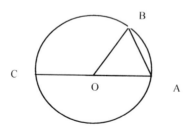

*__Answers for this section can be found on page 161__*

# Solid Geometry Warm Up

You're probably not going to see too many questions involving solid geometry. It's still worth it to know a few facts.

## Easy

1. The volume of a rectangular prism is 36 units$^3$.
   If the area of the base is 18 units$^2$, what is the height?

1. _____

## Medium

2. A rectangular prism has a volume of 24 in$^3$, and the area
   of the base is 6 in$^2$. If the lengths of all of the edges are integers
   greater than 1, what is its' surface area?

2. _____

## Hard

3. If a sphere were inscribed within a right circular cylinder
   so that the diameter of the sphere and the cylinder were equal,
   what would be the ratio of the volume of the sphere to the volume
   of the cylinder?

3. _____

# Solid Geometry Warm Up Solutions

## Easy
### 1.  2

The formula for the volume of a rectangular prism is V=(length)(width)(height).  The length and the width form the area of the base.  To find the height, use the formula 36=18h.  Solving this gives you a height of 2.

## Medium
### 2.  52

The surface area of a rectangular prism can be found using the formula SA=2 (lw+lh+wh).  Since the area of the base is 6 and all of the dimensions are integers greater than one, the length and width have to be 2 and 3.  Their order isn't important.

Given a volume of 24 and a base with an area of 6, the height would have to be 4.  Therefore the surface area would be SA=2(2*3+2*4+3*4)=52.

## Hard
### 3.  2/3

The volume of a sphere is found by the formula V= $\frac{4}{3}\pi r^3$ .  The volume of a cylinder is found by the formula V=πr²h.  If the sphere were inscribed within the cylinder, it would be tangent to the cylinder at the sides as well as the bases.  This means that the height of the cylinder would be equal to the diameter.  Letting the r=1, the sphere would have a volume of $\frac{4}{3}\pi$ and the cylinder would have a volume of 2π.  Simplifying the ratio leaves you with 2:3.

# Solid Geometry Facts

There are not that many solid geometry questions on the SAT but there are a few basic facts you need to know. Most are given on the formula bar in the front of each section.

1. The volume of a rectangular prism is V=(length)(width)(height)

2. The volume of a cylinder is $V=\pi r^2 h$

3. The sides of a prism are called the *faces*. The corners are called *vertices* (each one is called a *vertex*) and the line segments where two faces meet are called *edges*.

4. In a rectangular prism the length of a diagonal through the prism can be found using the equation $d^2=l^2+w^2+h^2$.

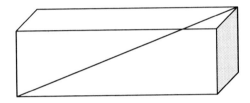

5. Surface are is the area of all of the exterior surfaces of the shape. It is measured in square units.

6. The equation for the surface area of a cube is $SA=6e^2$, where e= the length of an edge.

# Solid Geometry Problems

## Basic Questions

1. What is the volume of a rectangular prism whose length, width and height are 4, 5, and 6 feet respectively?

   1. _____

2. What is the volume of a cylinder whose radius is 4cm and whose height is 3 cm? (leave your answer in terms of $\pi$)

   2. _____

3. The area of the base of a rectangular prism is 16 cm$^2$ and the height is 5 cm. What is the volume of the prism?

   3. _____

## SAT Questions

4. The ratio of the volumes of two cubes are in a ratio of 8:27. What is the ratio of their surface area?
   a. 2:3
   b. 4:6
   c. 4:9
   d. 8:27
   e. Cannot be determined

   4. _____

5. You are given a cube whose volume is 64 cm$^3$. What is the distance from the center of the front face to one of the vertices on the rear face?
   a. 4
   b. 16
   c. $4\sqrt{10}$
   d. $16\sqrt{5}$
   e. $2\sqrt{6}$

   5. _____

6. The volume of a cube and a cylinder are the same. If the volume of the cylinder is $8\pi$ cm$^3$, what is the length of an edge of the cube?

6. _____

       *a.* $2\pi$

       *b.* $4\pi$

       *c.* $\dfrac{2}{\pi}$

       *d.* $\dfrac{2}{\pi^3}$

       *e.* $2\sqrt[3]{\pi}$

Grid Ins

7. A rectangular prism below has dimensions of 3 x 12 x 4. What is the length of the segment connecting A and B?

7. _____

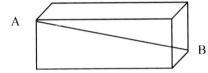

8. A cube whose volume is 125cm$^3$ is painted and then divided up into equally sized cubes whose volume is 1cm$^3$. How many of the smaller cubes are not painted?

8. _____

**Answers for this section can be found on page 163**

# Geometry Review

The following are examples of SAT style questions covering all areas of geometry. This section should be done after all of the other geometry sections have been completed.

1.  What is the length of the hypotenuse of the right triangle below?

    1.

    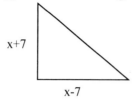

    x+7

    x-7

    *a.* $2x$

    *b.* $x^2 - 49$

    *c.* $\sqrt{2x^2 + 49}$

    *d.* $\sqrt{2x^2 + 98}$

    *e.* $\sqrt{x^2 + 49}$

2.  Using the diagram below, what is the value of y?

    2.

    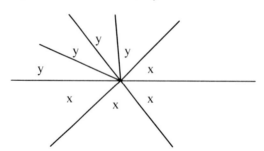

    a. 15
    b. 30
    c. 40
    d. 50
    e. 60

3.  A triangle with sides of integral lengths has exactly 2 equal sides. What is the smallest possible perimeter?

    3. _____

    a. 3
    b. 4
    c. 5
    d. 6
    e. Cannot be determined

4. If the perimeter of a rectangle were cut in half, its area would be:     4. _____
   a. divided by 8
   b. decreased by 8
   c. divided by 4
   d. decreased by 4
   e. cut in half

5. Which of the following could NOT be the lengths of the sides of a triangle?   5. _____
   a. 2,3,4
   b. 3,4,5
   c. 5,12,13
   d. 3,3,2
   e. 2,4,6

6. The areas of two circles are in a ratio of 1:4. Which could be the their     6. _____
   circumferences?
   a. π and 4π
   b. 2π and 4π
   c. π and 8π
   d. π and 16π
   e. Cannot be determined

7. In the picture below, lines A and B are parallel to each other. What is the     7. _____
   value of the angle marked x?

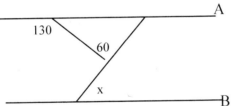

   a. 20
   b. 30
   c. 50
   d. 60
   e. 70

8. What is the perimeter of an equilateral triangle whose area is $4\sqrt{3}$ ?     8. _____
   a. 4
   b. 8
   c. 12
   d. 16
   e. 64

9. A rider on a bicycle rides 4 miles north, then 6 miles east. After a brief rest he 9. _____
goes another mile north and then 6 miles east. How far from his starting
place is he?

    a. 5miles

    b. 12 miles

    c. 13 miles

    d. 15 miles

    e. 17 miles

10. In rhombus ABCD below, the length of AB and BD are 4. What is the     10. _____
area of ABCD?

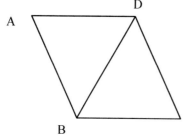

    *a.* **4**

    *b.* $4\sqrt{2}$

    *c.* $4\sqrt{3}$

    *d.* $8\sqrt{2}$

    *e.* $8\sqrt{3}$

11. Which expression represents the area of the rectangle in terms of x?     11. _____

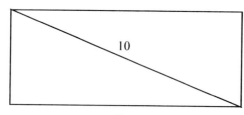

    *a.* $A = 10x$

    *b.* $A = 2x + 10 / x$

    *c.* $A = x^2 x$

    *d.* $A = x(10 - x)$

    *e.* $A = x\sqrt{100 - x^2}$

12. In the picture below, line segment AB is parallel to CD and ED is parallel    12. _____
    to FG. If the angle ABD measures 110° and GFD measures 120°, what is the
    measure of angle CDE?

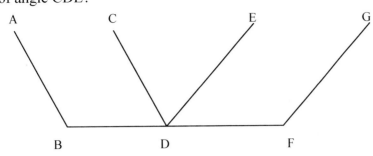

    a. 40
    b. 50
    c. 60
    d. 70
    e. 80

Grid Ins
13. Lines M and N are parallel to each other and segment AB bisects angle    13. _____
    CBD. If the measure of angle BDE is 140, what is the measure of
    angle BAD?

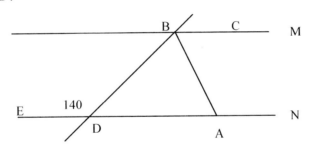

14. An exterior angle of a regular polygon has an angle of 40 degrees. What    14. _____
    is the measure of one of it's interior angles?

15. Starting with a square piece of paper, you will cut out the largest possible    15. _____
    circle and discard the remaining pieces. From that circle you will cut out
    the largest possible square and discard the remaining paper. What is the
    ratio of the areas of the final square paper to the original square piece of paper?

### _Answers for this section can be found on page 164_

# Appendix A:
# Problem Solutions

# Practice Solutions

## Pg. 13 Tactics: Picking Numbers

1. **C**; Let the length and width both be 10 (10 and 100 are the easiest numbers to use when working with percents). This would give you an area of 100. When the length and width were increased and decreased by 30% they would then be 13 and 7 giving a new area of 91 which is a 9% decrease.
2. **C**; Letting N=2, P=4 and Q=3 (they could be any numbers, but you want numbers that will be quick and easy) you can find that if 2 candy bars cost $4, then 3 candy bars would cost $6. Plug in 2, 4, and 3 for the variables and C is the only one that works.
3. **D**; If Tom saves $5 a week for 10 weeks he would have saved $50. Plugging these numbers into these choices, T=K/S.
4. **B**; If you let x=1, you would get 4. Plugging 1 into any other solution will not give you 4.
5. **E**; If N is 100, then there are 100 boys and 25 girls. This means that 100/125 or 80% of the school is boys. Plugging 100 in for N in the choices, gives you E.

## Pg. 15 Tactics: Using Choices

1. **D**; Test the choices and start with c. 25 cars would give you $200 dollars which is too high. Therefore work towards higher number of cars since this would lower the number of trucks which bring in more money.
2. **B;** Test the choices
3. **B**; Starting with C, if Sean had spent $120, then Evan would have spent $240 which is too high (Evan and Ryan spent a total of $210). This eliminates choices C, D and E. Testing B, if Sean spent $90, Evan spent $180 and Ryan spent $30. Since $180 and $30 add to $210 B is the correct choice.
4. **E**; Use the fractions. The number of students has to be a multiple of 5 and 3. Therefore, all the choices except 15 and 30 are eliminated. Then test each choice.
5. **B**; Use the fractions. The number of jellybeans has to be a multiple of 4 and 6. This eliminates all the choices except 12.

## Pg. 17 Various Strategies.

1. **C**; It's a pattern of 5 repeating numbers whose sum is 2. Dividing 129 by 5 gives 25 with a remainder of 4. The sum of the first 4 numbers in the pattern is 4. Therefore the sum is (25×2)+4=54.
2. **E**; Either substitute y/2 for x and do the algebra or pick a number for y.
3. **2**; Pick a number that will give a remainder of 2 when divided by 5. The smallest number is 7. Therefore, 6k=42. The remainder when 42 is divided by 5 is 2.
4. **14.3**; When doing percent problems, use good numbers (100 and 10 are best). If the solution is 100 grams, then 25 are alcohol and 75 are water. Doubling the water gives 150 grams of water and 25 of alcohol. Using the proportion is/of=%/100 gives you 14.3% alcohol.
5. **13**; The cyclist has gone a total of 12 miles north and 5 miles east. This forms a right triangle. Using Pythagorean Theorem, gives a distance of 13.
6. **3/10**; Pick good numbers. Z should be a number divisible by 4 and 5. Letting Z=20, then Y=8 and X=6. The ratio of x/z would by 6/20 or 3/10.

## Pg. 24 Arithmetic Facts

1. 2, 3, 5, 7
2. 2
3. 1, -3, 48/16
4. 1
5. 6
6. **D**; Pick numbers, but know your even-odd rules. Remember, there is no consistent rule for division!
7. **A**; N could be 1 or 2.
8. **B**; If m were 14 and n were 3, m+n is only choice that works.
9. **D**; a is 2 and b is 7.
10. **B**; If r or s were 1 then, t could be equal to the other. Watch out for FONZ traps.
11. **E**; We don't know the order of the points. Don't assume they are in alphabetical order.
12. **C**; Multiply each choice by 5. C is the only one that will not be an integer.
13. **C**; 74. Since both the first and last numbers are included, you have to subtract the numbers and add 1.
14. **B**; Pick numbers and test. Watch out for FONZ traps!!

15. **D**; Pick numbers and test each choice.
16. **11**; Let p=5 and q= -6.
17. **1**; Don't assume it had to be 3 and 7.
18. **29**; Do NOT do out all the arithmetic. Most numbers will cancel out from the subtraction leaving 15+14.

## Pg. 27 Even and Odd Problems
1. **D**; Pick numbers and know your rules. Choices A and B are out immediately because division is inconsistent.
2. **C**; 0, -2, and 48/3
3. **E**; Since x+y is even, x and y are both even or both odd. Pick numbers and test. Z is always odd.
4. **C**; You don't know anything about J and K individually . Since they add to an even number, they are both even or both odd. Either way J+K is even.
5. **E**; Pick numbers for the variables and test the choices.

## Pg. 33 Fractions, Decimals and Ratios
1. **x=3**
2. **x=5**
3. **27 feet**
4. **B**; The ratio of lefties to righties is 1/3:2/3 which reduces to 1/2.
5. **A**; Since the ratio is 3/5, then 3/8 of the total are Juniors. This is 37.5%
6. **B**; If 75% are rejected, then 25% are accepted. 25/75 reduces to 1/3.
7. **A**; The sum of the parts of the ratio is 8. Therefore, the total number must be divisible by 8.
8. **D**; Multiply both ratios by different numbers so that the value of B is the same. Using 5 and 2, you get ratios of a:b=10:25 and a:c=10:14. Canceling out the a's gives you a ratio of b:c=25:14.
9. **C**; You can pick numbers or use algebra. Remember that your answer has to be a fraction because the question asks what *part* of the job was finished on Saturday.
10. **3/7**; Beware of part to part and part to whole questions. There are 15 boys out of a total of 35 people.
11. **56**; Set up a proportion. (84/60minutes=x/40 minutes)
12. **26.5**; Set up a proportion. (168 m/3.5 h=1272m/x)
13. **28%**; There are 7 sophomores out of 25 people. 7/25=28%
14. **20/9**; This question is similar to question 9. Multiplying both equations and eliminating the B's gives us 9a=20c. This equation cannot be solved for either variable, but you can divide by c and 9 giving you a/c=20/9.
15. **110**; Right now there are 10 white balls out of a total of 70. The key to this question is NOT reducing the proportion because you are adding x ball to both the numerator and denominator. You will end up with the proportion: $\dfrac{10+x}{70+x} = \dfrac{2}{3}$

    Cross multiplying and solving for x gives you 110.

## Pg. 36 Fraction Questions
1. **37/21**
2. **1/16**
3. **5/3**
4. **1/(x-6)**; After the (x+6) cancels in the numerator and denominator, remember that the resulting (x-6) was in the denominator.
5. **(b+a)/(b-a)**; To simplify a complex fraction, multiply every term by the LCD (Lowest Common Denominator)
6. **84/31**
7. **B**; The equation is a proportion. You can flip over one side if you flip the other.
8. **A**; Any number divided by its opposite is –1.
9. **D**; Lots of traps here. Pick a number of CD's(20 is best) and work out the problem He gave away 11 CD's and kept 9 for himself. The ratio would be 9:11.
10. **5/4**; This question is similar to question 7. Cancel out all the fractions that are common to both sides. This leaves you with a proportion. Just flip each side over.
11. $X^3$, $X^2$,**X**; Just pick a number for x. This is a FONZ Trap!!

12. **17/2 or 8.5**; It helps to look at the numbers in this problem in a different way. Expressing each fraction as an improper fraction gives you $(3/2)(4/3)(5/4)....(17/16)$. When you multiply, most numerators and denominators will cancel out.

## Pg. 38 Tough (but easy) Fraction Problems

1. **2/5**; Pick a number of mice (15 is best) and work it out one fraction at a time. If you started with 15 you would have 6 still alive. $6/15 = 2/5$

2. **2/5**; Let the shirt be $60 and figure it out one fraction at a time. You would pay $24 for the shirt. $24/60$ reduces to $2/5$.

3. **7/16**; There are 4 people with an equal amount of shares. You have a man selling 1/2 his shares and another giving up 1/4. Letting each person start with 4 shares has the woman finishing with 7 of the 16 shares.

4. **180**; Using the fractions, you would start with 15 people at the conference (15 is the common denominator). At 2PM, 1/5 leave. 1/5 of 15 takes away 3 people leaving 12. At 3PM 1/3 of the remaining people left. This would take away 4 leaving 8. At 4PM, twice the amount of people who left at 1:00 left. This means that 6 people left leaving 2 of the original 15. From here use the proportion: $\frac{2}{15} = \frac{24}{x}$ Therefore, x=180.

5. **3/20**; Work backwards. If there were 3 green apples, there must have been 12 red. With a total of 15 apples, there were 5 oranges giving us a total of 20 pieces of fruit.

## Pg. 42 Percentages

1. **8**
2. **26.6**
3. **48**
4. **25**
5. **18**
6. **23**; A classic! Don't actually do it out. The numbers always flip. a% of b is always equal to b% of a.
7. **C**; The sale is a 25% off sale $(20/80=.25)$. 20% of 40 is 10, so the price would be decreased by $10.
8. **C**; If the sale is 15% off, then you are paying 85% of the original price. 340 is 85% of 400.
9. **E**; Multiply the percentages. $(.2)(.4)=(.1)(x)$
10. **C**; If they buy the guitars for $50 and mark them up 50%, the selling price will by $75 and the profit will be $25. $25 is 33 1/3% of $75.
11. **B**; Either pick numbers for P and Q or set up the proportion is/of=%/100.
12. **B**; If he were saving $100/month, then he's saving a total of $1200 for the year. If he takes off 2 months, then he has to save the same amount of money over the course of 10 months. $1200/10 give you $120 or a 20% increase.
13. **54**; To increase a number by 50%, multiply it by 1.5 (100% +50%). Doing this 4 times gives you 54.
14. **99**; From 60 to a 66 is a 10% increase. 10% of 90 is 9 giving the student a 99 average.

## Pg 44 Arithmetic Practice

1. **C**; This is a FONZ trap. When you divide by a number between 0 and 1 the absolute value of the number will be bigger.
2. **E**; Any number times 2 is even. The others could vary depending on whether x and y are odd or even.
3. **B**; A ratio is a comparison of a part to a part. A percentage is a part to a whole.
4. **C**; 150% of x is 1.5x. Increasing x by 1.5x gives you 2.5x
5. **D**; Dividing 82 by 4 gives you 20.5. This is the exact middle of the 4 consecutive integers. Working outwards from here gives you 19,20,21, and 22.
6. **C**; This is a YO-YO Trap. When you go up and down by the same percentage, you will ALWAYS finish with less than what you started with. Letting d=100, going down by 10% would give you 90. Increasing this number by 10% brings you to 99. Therefore, the answer is .99d.
7. **E**; Multiply both equations so that the coefficient of b is the same. Using 5 and 4 would give you 15a=20b and 20b=24c. Now that the b's are the same you can eliminate them giving you 15a=24c. Dividing both sides by 15c gives you a/c=24/15 which reduces to 8/5.
8. **C**; This is a pattern of 5 numbers whose sum is 2 that repeats infinitely. Dividing 137 by 5 gives you 27 with a remainder of 2. Therefore you have 27 2's and the first 2 number of sequence add to 3. 27(2)+3=57.

10. **E;** Using the problems we get that t=2n-m. Solving this for m we get m=2n-t. When you find the value of n+3m, substitute (2n-t) for m giving you n+3(2n-t). This simplifies to 7n-2t.

11. **B;** All of the numbers have 2 distinct prime factors except 8. $8=2^3$

12. **48;** 30% of 40 is 12. 12 is 25% of 48.

13. **18;** Pick numbers for the variables. A faster way would be to recognize that (ac+cb+bc-ad) = (a+b)(c-d).

14. **3/20 or .15;** Using the denominators, assume there are 60 people in the club. Using this, there are 20 seniors and 40 juniors. Of the seniors there are 5 boys and 15 girls. Therefore, there are a total of 36 boys leaving 9 junior girls. 9/60 simplifies to 3/20.

15. **5;** Rewrite each expression as an improper fractions. You get (3/2)(4/3)(5/4)......(10/9). From here you can see that the numerators and denominators of the fractions would cancel leaving you with 10/2 or 5.

## Pg. 51  Equations and Inequalities

1. **6**

   | 2x+6=4x-6 | Subtract 2x from both sides |
   | 6=2x-6 | Add 6 to both sides and divide by 2 |
   | x=6 | |

2. **4 and –12;** Absolute value equations could have 2 answers. Step one is to isolate the absolute value. Then split the equation into the positive and negative cases.

   $$\longleftarrow \;|x+4|=8\; \longrightarrow$$

   | x+4=8 | x+4= -8 | Now solve |
   | x=4 | x=-12 | |

3. **-5 and 2;** Factoring the equation gives us (x+5)(x-2)=0. Since either factor could be zero, your solutions could be –5 or 2.

4. **62;** To solve a radical equation, you must first isolate the radical by adding 3 to both sides. Once this is done square both sides to give you x+2=64. Solving gives us x=62.

5. **x<3;** Solve and inequality the same way you would an equation.

   | 2(x-3)<3-x | Distribute the 2 |
   | 2x-6<3-x | Add x to both sides |
   | 3x-6<3 | Add 6 to both sides and divide by 3 |
   | x<3 | |

6. **D;** The graph of a function will touch the x axis where the y value is 0. Setting the equation to 0 give you

   | $x^2+2x-24=0$ | Factor |
   | (x+6)(x-4)=0 | Solve for x |
   | x= -6    x=4 | |

7. **A;** The key to these types of questions is to make the bases the same. Remember that $4=2^2$

   | $4^{x+2}=2^{x-1}$ | |
   | $(2^2)^{x+2}=2^{x-1}$ | |
   | $2^{2x+4}=2^{x-1}$ | Once the bases are the same, the exponents must be equal |
   | 2x+4=x-1 | Solve for x |
   | x= -5 | |

8. **E;** If the roots are equal to each other, it means the discriminant is equal to 0.

   $$b^2-4ac=0$$
   $$(8)^2-4(1)(k)=0$$
   $$64-4k=0$$
   $$k=16$$

9. **B;** Evaluating the function gives us x(x+4)=21. Distributing the x gives us the quadratic equation $x^2+4x=21$. Remember that a quadratic equation has to be set equal to zero.

   | $x^2+4x-21=0$ | Now factor. |
   | (x+7)(x-3)=0 | Solve each for x |
   | x= -7    x=3 | |

10. **C;** The roots of the equation are 6 and k. Since the sum of the roots is –b/a, we get the equation 6+k=3k Solving for k gives us k=3.

11. **C;** The quickest way to get this is to simply test the choices. -1 is the only one that doesn't work.

12. **E;** If this were a grid in question, you would have to isolate one radical, square both sides and then isolate and square both sides again. Luckily, you can test the choices. Save time by eliminating numbers that won't form perfect squares in the radicals.

13. **B**; If John can finish in 4 hours it means he does 1/4 of the job every hour. Tom finishes 1/6 of the job per hour. Letting x represent the time they work together we get the equation (1/4)x+(1/6)x=1. Multiply the equation by 24. This gives you 6x+4x=24. Solving for x gives you x=2.4 hours.

14. **D**; The middle of the range of temperatures is –35 and both of the temperatures are 25 degrees from the middle. Remember the format |x-middle|<distance. This gives us |x-(-35)|<25 or |x+35|<25.

## Pg. 56 Exponents and Roots

1. $-8x^2y$
2. $25x^4y^8$
3. $15^{3x}$
4. $15^4$
5. $2^7$
6. $4a^2$
7. $5\sqrt{2}$
8. $4\sqrt{5}$

9. **D**; When you multiply terms with the same base, you add the exponents. III is equal to $2^{5x}$.
10. **D**; Choice III doesn't work.
11. **E**; Since the answer is a whole number, x must be a perfect square.
12. **A**; Reduce the expression using your exponential rules. $64a=8^2a=(a^x)^2a^1$. Using your exponent rules, this expression is equal to $a^{2x+1}$.
13. **D**; Advanced students will be tempted to use logarithms here-DON'T. Use your exponent rules. $2^{x+2}=(2^x)(2^2)$. Therefore, you would get (3)(4)=12
14. **15**; Using exponent rules m+3=14 and 3n=12. Therefore, m=11 and n=3.
15. **12**; Multiplying out $9^3$ and $27^2$ gives you 531,441. This is $3^{12}$. Using exponent rules, $9^3=(3^2)^3=3^6$. Also, $27^2=(3^3)^2=3^6$. Multiplying both of these gives you $3^{12}$.
16. **25/4**; This one is similar to the last one. $4^{x-1}=(2^2)^{x-1}=2^{2x-2}$ Remember your exponent rules. Subtraction of exponents is caused by division. So $2^{2x-2}=2^{2x}/2^2=(2^x)^2/2^2$. Using that $2^x=5$, we get $5^2/2^2=25/4$

## Pg. 62 Polynomials and Factoring

1. $(x+6)(x-6)$
2. $(10+w)(10-w)$
3. $(x+4)(x+4)$
4. $(x^2+9)(x+3)(x-3)$
5. $x^2+6x+9$
6. $x^2-y^2$
7. $16-x^2$
8. $x^2 + 2x\sqrt{5} + 5$

9. **A**; This factors to $\sqrt{(x+y)^2}$ which is equal to (x+y). Substituting 3x for y gives you 4y.
10. **D**; Starting with the equation $kx^2+y=ky^2+x$ isolate the terms with k on one side.

$$kx^2-ky^2=x-y \qquad \text{Factor out k}$$
$$k(x^2-y^2)=x-y \qquad \text{Divide by } x^2-y^2$$
$$k = \frac{x-y}{x^2-y^2} \qquad \text{Factor and simplify}$$
$$k = \frac{1}{x+y}$$

11. **3**; Factoring gives you (x+y)(x-y)=24. Since (x+y)=8, (x-y) must be 3.
12. **8**; $(a^2-b^2)$ factors to (a+b)(a-b). Dividing out, the (a+b)'s cancel out leaving you with a-b=8.
13. **8**; $(x+y)^2$ multiplies out to $x^2+2xy+y^2$. Since $x^2+y^2=20$ you can substitute this giving you 20+2xy=36. Solving for xy gives you 8. Remember, don't bother solving for x or y separately.
14. **1**; C is the coefficient of x. Save time here by multiplying out only the terms that will give x's. 3(-3x)+2(5x)=1x.
15. **4**; Multiply out the binomials. $(x+4)^2=x^2+8x+16$. $(x+6)(x+2)=x^2+8x+12$. The first product is 4 units bigger.

16. **5**; This is an example of a special polynomials question. Taking the equation:

$$x^2+y^{-2}-16=9-2xy \qquad \text{Isolate the variables}$$
$$\underline{+2xy \; +16 \;\; +16 \; +2xy}$$
$$x^2+2xy+y^2=25 \qquad \text{Factor}$$
$$(x+y)^2=25 \qquad \text{Take the square root of both sides}$$
$$(x+y)=5$$

17. **30**; This isn't really a factoring question but it looks like one. Since $x^2+x=12$ the tendency of most people would be to set the equation equal to zero and solve. However, $3x^2+3x-6$ can be rewritten as $3(x^2+x)-6$. Knowing that $x^2+x=12$, allows you to substitute giving you $3(12)-6=30$.

## Pg. 68 Systems of Equations

1. **x=2**        **y=-1**
2. **x=38**      **y=-28**
3. **Soda=$2**    **Hotdog=$3.50**
4. **B**; These are your special polynomials. $R=x+y$ and $S=x-y$. Subtracting gives you $2y$.
5. **9**; Add the equations.
6. **12**; Subtract the equations
7. **9**; Adding the equations gives you $5x+5y$. From here, you can divide by 5 to get $x+y=3$. Therefore, $3x+3y=9$.
8. **18**; A system of equations will have an infinite number of solutions if the two equations form lines that overlap. When reduced to $y=mx+b$ form, they are the same equation.
9. **5**; Setting up a system of equations we would get:

$$B+R=12$$
$$R+G=14$$
$$\underline{B+G=8}$$
$$2B+2G+2R=34 \qquad \text{Divide everything by 2}$$
$$B+G+R=17$$

We know from the first equation that $B+R=12$. Subtracting this from $B+G+R=17$ gives us $G=5$.

## Pg. 74 Averages

1. **2x+4**; Add the terms and divide by 3
2. **20**; Since the average is 10 the five numbers must add up to 50. The 4 known numbers add to 30. So the fifth must be 20.
3. **6**; Adding up the frequency, there are 9 numbers. By multiplying each score by the frequency and adding up the results you will find that the 9 numbers add to 54. 54/9=6
4. **6**; Median is the middle number when they are listed in order.
5. **C**; There are 2 numbers whose average is A, so the total of the numbers is 2A. Subtracting A gives you 2A-B.
6. **E**; You can't add terms with different exponents. The sum of the two numbers is $(2^{10}+2^{20})$. Finding their average, you would have to divide this by 2. When you divide terms with the same base, you subtract their exponents.
7. **C**; As soon as you add any of the 50% mixture to the 30% mixture, the result will be between 30% and 50 %.
8. **90**; This is a classic "Before-After" Question. Multiplying the number of scores and the average gives you the total number of points. Before there had been 320 points scored. After, there were 410. The difference was the 5th test.
9. **75**; This is a slightly harder "Before-After" Question. Before there had been 320 points scored. After 7 tests there had been 595. The difference was 275 points over 3 tests. If the 5th test was the lowest, the others must have been the highest. Letting the highest scores be 100, you get a lowest possible score of 75.
10. **12.5**; Again, this a "Before-After" Question. There are 6 numbers with an average of 15 so the total is 90. The high and low have an average of 20 so their total is 40. Finding the difference we see that the total of the remaining 4 numbers is 50. 50/4 is 12.5.
11. **153**; Read this one carefully. Five integers with an average of 98 will have a total of 490. Subtracting 58 and 76 gives you 356. This is where you have to be careful. The numbers are *different* and all *over 100*. The lowest of the 3 remaining numbers had to be 101 and 102. The means the largest of the numbers had to be 153.
12. **2/1**; This is a very difficult question. It could be done as a "Before-After" question where algebraically you are trying to solve for P/N. There is an easier way. Rule 3 on page 48 states that the total deviation above and below the mean has to be the same. Since the average is 90, P must be bigger than N. Looking at the differences in the deviations of the 2 classes, you can see that the class of P students' average is 4 from the total average. The class of N students' average is 8 units from the total average. Using the equation 4P=8N gives you P/N=2/1.
13. **55**; Averaging 60 miles per hour for 3 hours means you have to cover 180 miles. If you went 70 miles per hour for the first hour, you've still got 110 miles to go and 2 hours to do it. 110/2=55.

## Pg. 80 Functions

1. **15**; f(3)=4(3)+3
2. **-3,2**; Let $x^2+x=6$. This gives you the equation $x^2+x-6=0$. Solving gives you x=-3 and x=2.
3. **X≥ 2**; You can't take the square root of a negative number.
4. **-14≤y≤10**; It's a linear function so the high and low elements of the range will correspond with the high and low of the domain.
5. **E**; The only function that will be the same regardless of whether the input is positive or negative is E.
6. **C**; Tricky question. Most people think this is the same as #4 on the same page but its' not because this function will form a parabola when graphed. The lowest possible value of y is when x=0. The highest is when x=3.
7. **B**; Plug g(x) into f(x) and simplify.
8. **C**; The function is already starting 2 units to the left and 3 units down. Going another 2 left changes (x+2) to (x+4) and the -3 will go down to -7.
9. **C**; To evaluate a function graphically, you are finding the y coordinate that corresponds with the given x value. When x=-2, then y=2. Therefore, f(-2)=2. Finding the f(f(-2)) means that the answer for f(-2) is going back into f(x). That is why the f is repeated. Using the 2 you got from the f(-2), when x=2, y=-1.
10. **D**; The question is asking ,where f(x)<0. Remember that f(x) is the same as y, so they are asking where the graph is below 0 or below the x axis. The happens to the left of A(-4,0) and between the origin and D(4,0). The interval is (x<-4)∧(0x<4).
11. **C**; f(x+2)-2 means that f(x) is shifted 2 units left and 2 down. The easiest way to do this problem is to simply let x=-4. Therefore g(-4)=f(-4+2)-2. Using the graph, f(-2)=2. Decreasing this by 2 gives you 0.

12. **A**; You can't have a negative number under a radical and the radical is in the denominator of a fraction so it can't be zero either.

13. **2.5 or 5/2**; The SAT loves to create symbols that define random operations. Plugging in 5 for a gives you the proportion

$$\frac{5+b}{5-b} = \frac{3}{1} \qquad Cross\,multiply$$

$$3(5-b) = 5+b \qquad Distribute$$

$$15-3b = 5+b \qquad Solve$$

$$4b = 10$$

$$b = 10/4 = 5/2$$

14. **1**; The key to this question is using the fact that f(5)=13 to solve for k. Plugging 5 in for x and letting f(x)=4 gives you $(5)^2$-3(5)+k=13. Solving for k gives you k=3. Evaluating f(2) will give you 1.

15. **9**; When two numbers vary inversely they multiply to a constant. Since x=6 when y=6 that constant is 36. Therefore, 4y=36 and y=9

16. **1, 2, or 3**; Use the inequality $x^2$-2x<8. Setting this equal to zero will give us $x^2$-2x-8<0. From here:

$$(x-4)(x+2)<0 \qquad Factor\ and\ solve$$

$$4 \quad -2 \qquad Find\ the\ roots$$

Keep in mind that these numbers are the roots of the quadratic equation. Testing numbers between them, we see that all the numbers work, but the question states that x is a positive integer.

## Pg. 86 Sequences

1. **E**; Expand the pattern out a few terms to see if there is any repetition. Following the rule of the pattern we get:

4, 6, -6, -4, 4, 6, -6, ......

There is a pattern of 4 numbers repeated. Dividing 55 by 4 gives you 13.75. The remainder is represented by .25. You have to convert this into a fraction with a denominator of 4 since there are four numbers in the pattern. .75=3/4. Therefore, the 55th term is the 3rd of the 4 numbers.

2. **4**; The sum of the first 4 numbers is 0. Dividing 11 by 4 gives us 2.75. The .75 is equivalent to 3/4 meaning you have to use 3 of the 4 terms. The sum of the first 3 terms is 4.

3. **6**; These questions are very common. There is a pattern of 4 repeating numbers. Do NOT count out 43 terms!! Simply divide 43 by 4. You get 10 with a remainder of 3. This means that you will repeat the pattern 10 times and have 3 terms left over. For this question, the 3 is the important part. The 3rd term in the sequence is 6 so the 43rd term is 6.

4. **254**; Since the terms increase by 3 each time, this is an arithmetic sequence. Use the formula $a_n$=$a_1$+d(n-1) where d=3, n=85 and $a_1$=3. Substituting your values you would get:

$$a_{85}=2+3(85-1)$$

$$a_{85}=2+282$$

$$a_{85}=284$$

5. **135**; Also an arithmetic sequence. Its decreasing by 3 each time.

$$a_{49}=9-3(49-1)$$

$$a_{29}= -135 \text{ The absolute value is 135.}$$

6. **3.5 or 7/2**; The entire sequence of wood is 2 feet long. Dividing 13 feet by 2 gives you 6.5. This means that you will repeat the pattern 6 and 1/2 times. Oak is in the first half of the sequence so it will get used 7 times.

7. **63**; Use the given information to find the value of d.

$$a_{12}=a_1+d(n-1)$$

$$51=7+d(12-1)$$

$$44=11d$$

$$d=4$$

Knowing the value of d lets you use the formula one more time to find the 15th term.

8. **6**; Most calculators won't give you a usable answer. (If your does, use it!!). When a problem asks you to find a term so late in a sequence, it is usually a time trap. Try to find a pattern.

$$2^1=2 \quad 2^2=4 \quad 2^3=8 \quad 2^4=16$$

$$2^5=32 \quad 2^6=64 \quad 2^7=128 \quad 2^8=256$$

Looking at the units digits, you can see that there is a pattern of 2, 4, 8, 6, .... Since there are 4 numbers in the pattern, divide 100 by 4. The remainder tells us what number in the pattern we finish on. Since the remainder is 0, the 100th term is the last number in the pattern.

9. **27/4;** This is a geometric sequence because you are multiplying by .75 each time. You are only looking for the 4th term so expand it out: 16, 12, 9, 27/4

## Pg. 88 Algebra Review

1. **E;** The average of two terms is their sum divided by 2. Since you can't add terms with different exponents, you have $(2^8+2^{12})/2$. The bases are 2 so you can divide them. When you divide terms with the same base and different exponents, you subtract exponents. Remember, if an exponent isn't shown its understood to be 1. This gives you $2^7+2^{11}$.

2. **A;**

$$\frac{s}{t} = \frac{x}{y} + 1 \qquad \textit{Isolate the x and y}$$

$$\frac{s}{t} = \frac{x}{y} + \frac{y}{y} \qquad \textit{Combine}$$

$$\frac{s}{t} = \frac{x+y}{y} \qquad \textit{Take the reciprocal of both sides}$$

$$\frac{t}{s} = \frac{y}{x+y}$$

When solving a problem like this, it is important to note that you can only take the reciprocals of both sides when the equation is a proportion. This is why you have to combine terms first.

3. **C;** Absolute value represents a distance. The form for an absolute value inequality like this is:

**|x-(average)|<Distance of high (or low) from average**

The average of the weights is 153, and the highest and lowest weights are 57 pounds away from this. You would say "The weights are less than 57 pounds from 153."

4. **C;** $(x+4)(x-4)=x^2-16$. Therefore, p must be $-16/x$.

5. **C;** A negative exponent flips its base over therefore you have:

$$\frac{x+y}{1} = \frac{1}{x-y}$$

Cross multiplying this gives you $x^2-y^2=1$.
Letting x=3 brings you to $9-y^2=1$. Therefore $y^2=8$ and y= $\pm 2\sqrt{2}$

6. **B;** The key to average questions is finding the total. The average of 3 numbers is their sum divided by 3. The median (middle) is y to we have the equation

$$\frac{x+y+z}{3} = 3y \quad \textit{The average of 3 numbers is their sum divided by 3}$$
$$x+y+z = 9y \quad \textit{Cross multiply}$$
$$x+z = 8y$$
$$\frac{x+z}{2} = 4y \quad \begin{array}{l}\textit{Subtract y from each side}\\\textit{Dividing both sides by 2 finds the average of x and z}\end{array}$$

To make the average of x and z equal to the average of x, y, and z you would have to multiply by 4/3.

7. **7/3;** Cancel out all the terms that are similar to both sides of the equation. This will leave you with 1/x=3/7. Taking the reciprocal of both sides gives you x=3/7.

8. **5;** These are operations that are made up but very similar to a composition of two functions. X*=x-1. When you then evaluate (x-1)# you get $(x-1)^2-1$ which is $(x^2-2x+1)-1$ or $x^2-2x$. Then you use the equation:

$$\begin{array}{ll} x^2-2x=15 & \textit{Set equal to 0}\\ x^2-2x-15=0 & \textit{Factor}\\ (x-5)(x+3)=0 & \textit{Solve}\\ x=5 \quad x=-3 & \textit{Take positive solutions}\end{array}$$

9. **12;** Make sure you know your special factors. $(x+y)^2=x^2+2xy+y^2$. Since $(ax+b)=4x^2+12x+c$ we can conclude that a=2. The middle term is always twice the product of the last and first terms. 2(2x)(b)=12x. Since b=3 and c=9, then b+c=12

10. **30**; This is similar to the last problem. Since $(rx+t)^2=9x^2+px+25$ we know that $r=3$ and $t=5$. The middle term is equal to twice the product of the first and last terms of the binomial that is squared. $2(3x)(5)=30x$.

11. **1/2**; Since there are two variables with only one equation, it will be impossible to find the actual values of either. That is why this question asks for the ratio of x to y.

$$4x+12=2y+6+6 \qquad \textit{Distribute}$$
$$4x+12=2y+12 \qquad \textit{Combine like terms}$$
$$4x=2y \qquad \textit{Subtract 12 from both sides}$$
$$(4x)/y=2 \qquad \textit{Divide both sides by y}$$
$$x/y=2/4 \qquad \textit{Divide by 4 and reduce}$$

12. **5/9**; The link between the freshmen and juniors is the sophomores. Multiplying the first ratio by 5 and the second ratio by 3 gives you the ratios 10 freshmen:15 sophomores and 15 sophomores:18 juniors. Eliminating the sophomores gives you 10 freshmen:18 juniors which reduces to 5:9.

13. **4**; Use the averages to help find the totals. Since the average is 6, $a+b+c+d=24$. the average of a and b is 10 so $a+b=20$. Subtracting the two equations gives you $c+d=4$.

14. **14**; This question is similar to the last one but a little harder. Using the averages to find totals, we get:

$$s+t+v+w=48$$
$$\underline{\quad s+t=16} \qquad \textit{Subtract the equations}$$
$$v+w=32$$

Now you have to use the fact that v is 4 more than w. Therefore we have that $v=w+4$. Substituting this into our last equation we bet $(w+4)+w=32$. Solving this gives you $w=14$.

15. **16**; Know the special factors!! $x^2-y^2=(x+y)(x-y)$.
$$x^2+2xy+y^2=(x+y)(x+y)$$
$$x^2-2xy+y^2(x-y)(x-y)$$

Since, $x^2+2xy+y^2=(x+y)(x+y)=81$, $x+y=9$. We were also given that $x^2-y^2=36$. Since this is $(x+y)(x-y)$ and we already know that $(x+y)=9$, then $x-y=4$. Therefore, $x^2-2xy+y^2$ which equals $(x-y)(x-y)=16$.

16. **12**; Add the two equations together. This gives you $5x+5y=30$. Dividing this by 5 gives you $x+y=6$. Therefore $2x+2y=12$. Remember, solving for the variable is not important. Solve for the expression.

## Pg. 95 Lines and Angles

1. **20**; The sum of the angles on a straight line is 180 degrees. Therefore, $4x+5x=180$.

2. **4**; Vertical angles are the non-adjacent angles formed when two lines intersect. The measures of vertical angles are equal giving us the equation $5x=2x+12$. Solving this equation gives us $x=4$.

3. **33**; When 2 parallel lines are intersected by a transversal (a 3rd non-parallel line) any pair of angles are either congruent or supplementary. Looking at the angles, one is obtuse and the other is acute so they must be supplementary. This gives us the equation:

$$2x+12+3x+3=180 \qquad \textit{Combine like terms}$$
$$5x+15=180 \qquad \textit{Solve for x}$$
$$5x=165$$
$$x=33$$

4. **9**; These angles are congruent to each other. This gives us the equation:

$$6x-24=2x+12 \qquad \textit{Subtract 2x and add 24 to both sides}$$
$$4x=36 \qquad \textit{Solve for x}$$
$$x=9$$

5. **20**; Complimentary angles add up to 90 degrees. Therefore:

$$2x+7x=90$$
$$9x=90$$
$$x=10$$

Be careful because the question doesn't ask to solve for x but asks the measure of the smaller angle which is 2x or 20 degrees.

6. **12**; Angles that are bisected are cut in half. Therefore,

$$3x+6=1/2(84)$$
$$3x+6=42$$
$$3x=36$$
$$x=12$$

7.  **B**;  The supplement of an angle is (180-x) and the complement of an angle is (90-x).  Put the equation together one phrase at a time:

"The supplement is 50 more than twice the complement"

$$(180-x) = 50 + 2 (90-x)$$

8.  **E**;  You can't assume that the order of the points is ABC.  The could also be CAB or BCA.  Therefore, the distance from A to C cannot be determined.

9.  **E**;  The sum of the angles on a straight line must be 180°. This gives us m<ABD+m<ABE+m<EBC=180.

m<ABE+m<CBD=260     Divide the angles into their parts

m<ABD+m<DBE+m<DBE+m<EBC=260   Subtract the straight line

-(<ABD+m<ABE+m<EBC=180)

m<DBE=80

10. **D**;  Use the triangle.  The angle in the triangle opposite *a* is a vertical angle, so the measure is 50.  The  angle in the triangle adjacent to *b* is its supplement so will have a measure of 60.  Since the angles of a triangle will add up to 180 degrees, the measure of angle *c* must be 70.

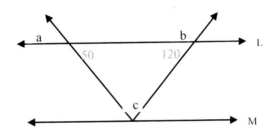

11. **C**;  The key here is to use the corresponding angles formed by the parallel lines with the triangle.  Use the alternate interior angle to 108 and adjacent angle to 130 to find two angles of the triangle.

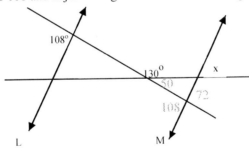

180-(72+50)=58

12. **C**;  Using the drawing 3x+(5x-12)=180.  Solving this, we get x=24.  We can also use 3x+y=180.  If x=24, then y=108.  Therefore, x+y=132.

13. **126≤x≤134**;  The picture is not drawn to scale and DBC is between 45 and 55 degrees.  This means that angle ABC is obtuse.  Angles ABD and DBC are alternate interior angles and x will be supplementary to DBC. Since ABD is between 45 and 55, the measure of DBC is also between 45 and 55.  Therefore, x must be between the supplements of these angles which are 126 and 134.

14. **20**;  Draw a line and label the points.

| | 1.5(.4x) | .4x | x | |
|---|---|---|---|---|
| A | | B | C | D |

Solving the equation .6x+.4x+x=40 gives us x=20.

15. **76**; AC and DB are parallel to each other. That means that DB is a transversal and x is the supplement of 104 which is 76.

16. **540**; It's impossible to find the value of x or y separately, but if you combine the two, you go once around a single point and you have a straight line. A circle (360) and a line (180) adds up to 540.

## Pg. 103 Triangles

1. **Longest=19**; (13+7)-1=19
   **Shortest=7**: (13-7)+1=7

2. **40**; The sum of the angles of a triangle is 180. Therefore:
$$2x+3x+4x=180$$
$$9x=180$$
$$x=20$$
   Since the smallest angle is 2x, the smallest angle is 40.

3. **23**; Using vertical angles, the missing angle of the triangle is 60. This gives us the equation:
   The angles of a triangle total 180.

   $3x+2x+5+60=180$     *Combine like terms*
   $5x+65=180$     *Subtract 65 from both sides*
   $5x=115$     *Solve for x*
   $x=23$

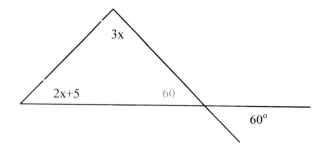

4 a. $8\sqrt{2}$ ; Using Pythagorean Theorem we get $8^2+8^2=128$. The square root of 128 is $8\sqrt{2}$
   b. **8**; Use Pythagorean Theorem

5. **D**; The Pythagorean Theorem says that if given a right triangle the sides will fit the relationship $a^2+b^2=c^2$ where a and b are the legs and c is the hypotenuse. Therefore, in a triangle, if $a^2+b^2=c^2$ the triangle must be right. Using this relation ship we can infer:
$$a^2+b^2>c^2 \text{ the triangle is acute}$$
$$a^2+b^2<c^2 \text{ the triangle is obtuse}$$
   Since, $4^2+5^2<7^2$ the triangle must be obtuse

6. **D**; A square is a clue that a 45-45-90 triangle is involved. Drawing the diagonal of the square creates the two triangles and the diagonal is also the diameter of the circle. Knowing the area of the square is 64 means the side of the square is 8 making the diagonal $8\sqrt{2}$ and the radius $4\sqrt{2}$

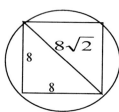

   From here, use the formula for the area of a circle ($A=\pi r^2$) to get $32\pi$ .

7. **E**; Because the perimeter of the square is 40 each side is 10 and its area is 100. The formula for the area of a equilateral triangle given its side (s) is:
$$A = \frac{s^2\sqrt{3}}{4}$$

154

Using this formula, the area of the triangle will be $\dfrac{10^2 \sqrt{3}}{4} = 25\sqrt{3}$

The area of the shaded region will be: $100 - 25\sqrt{3}$

Remember not to combine unlike terms.

8. **D**; Triangle ABC is equilateral. This means that each angle measures 60 degrees. Dropping altitude AE to

CB with form two 30-60-90 triangles. Using this fact the length of CE is 5 and AE is $5\sqrt{3}$
Altitude AE also bisects angle D. This forms two 45-45 90 triangles. Since CE is 5, DE is also 5. The length of AD will be $5\sqrt{3} - 5$

9. **E**; It's tempting to let the sides of the triangle be 1, 2 and 3. Remember that the smallest two sides of a triangle

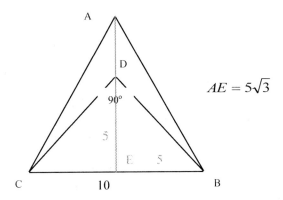

$AE = 5\sqrt{3}$

have to add up to more than the 3rd side. Since 2+3> 4, the smallest possible perimeter is 9.

10. **B**; The key to this question is to move around the sides. Slide AB over to CD and slide BC down. This will form an isosceles right triangle whose hypotenuse is 10. The reason it's isosceles is that AB+DC=BC. When given the hypotenuse of an isosceles right triangle the leg will be half the side of the triangle multiplied by the square root of two.

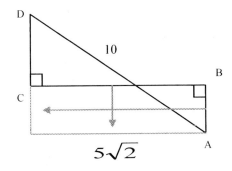

$5\sqrt{2}$

11. **E**; This problem has a little bit of everything.  Using Pythagorean Theorem,
$$(AD)^2 + (DC)^2 = (AC)^2$$
$$6^2 + (DC)^2 = 10^2$$
$$DC = 8$$

Knowing the 3,4,5 triplet is a time saver here.  Triangle BCD is a 30-60-90 triangle.  CB must be 16 and CD must be $8\sqrt{3}$ This question can be answered without actually doing the problem.  If you know that a

30-60-90 triangle involves a radical 3 you can eliminate choices a, b and d.  Knowing that whole numbers cannot be combined with irrational numbers, choice c can be eliminated leaving only e.

12. **C**;  Most people will mistakenly answer B thinking the sides would be 1, 1, 2.  This is wrong because any two sides of a triangle must add to more than the length of the 3rd side.  The smallest integral length of the sides are 2, 2, and 1.

13. **60**; Whether the triangle is obtuse or acute is irrelevant. The sum of the angles is always 180 degrees.  Dividing 180 by 3 gives you an average of 60.

14. **15**;  The most common wrong answer here is 9.  The reason this is wrong is that the smallest two sides of a triangle must add up to more than the 3rd.  1+3 is not more than 5.  However, 3+5>7 so these are the smallest possible sides.

15. **20**; The interior triangle has one angle with a a measure of 100.  Since the sum of the angles of a triangle add up to 180, the other two angles must total 80.  The large triangle has two base angles of (a+b).  This gives you the equation:

| | |
|---|---|
| (a+b)+(a+b)+x=180 | Substitute 80 for (x+b) |
| 80+80+x=180 | Solve for x |
| x=20 | |

16. **35**; If two angles form a straight line, they add up to 180.  Therefore, the angle adjacent to 130 has a measure of 50.  This gives us a triangle with two angles of 25 and 50.  Since the angles of a triangle add to 180, the missing side has a measure of 105.  Vertical angles are always equal to each other so the angle opposite 105 is also 105.  This give us a triangle with two angles of 40 and 105.  The missing angle must be 35 degrees.

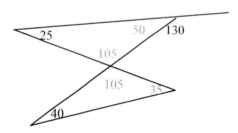

17. **17**; This is a very common question involving Pythagorean Triplets.  Draw out all the routes the rider took.

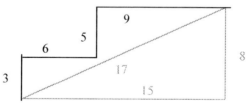

The key to the problem is looking at the total distances.  He went 15 miles East and 8 miles North.  The is the 8, 15, 17 triplet.

18. **15**; If two triangles share an adjacent side the ratios of their areas will be equal to the ratio of their bases.  The bases of the triangles are in a 3:5 ratio.
$$3x+5x=40$$
$$8x=40$$
$$x=5$$

Therefore the area of the smaller triangle is 3(5)=15 and the larger is 5(5)=25.

## Pg. 112 Coordinate Geometry

1.  $4\sqrt{12} = 4\sqrt{4}\sqrt{3} = 4(2)(\sqrt{3}) = 8\sqrt{3}$

2.  **-1**; Use the slope formula $\dfrac{y_2 - y_1}{x_2 - x_1}$     *Plugging in the coordinates gives us*

    $\dfrac{6-2}{-1-3}$     *This simplifies to* $-1$

3.  **(3,1)**; The midpoint is the average of the coordinates. (1+5)/2=3 and (-7+5)=-1 so the coordinates of the mid-point are (3, -1).

4.  $3\sqrt{5}$  Plugging the coordinates into the distance formula you would get:

    $$d = \sqrt{(6-0)^2 + (1-4)^3}$$
    $$d = \sqrt{45} = \sqrt{9}\sqrt{5}$$
    $$d = 3\sqrt{5}$$

5.  **(7,7)** ;  The best way to do questions like these is to draw them out.  The midpoint is always equidistant from the two endpoints.  Therefore, find the distance from the given midpoint and add that distance to the midpoint to find the other midpoint.

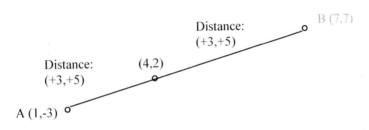

6.  **B**; Using the coordinates given, each side of the square is 3 units long.  The coordinates given form a vertical line segment so the other vertices must be 3 units in a horizontal direction.

7.  **C**, The x coordinates of vertical lines are all the same and the y coordinates of horizontal lines are also the same.

8.  **D**; The center of the circle is the origin which is the point (0,0).  Since is goes through the point (6, -8), the radius has a length of 10.

9.  **A**; Use the slope formula with the given coordinates to set up the proportion show below

    $\dfrac{k-2}{4-x} = \dfrac{-1}{2}$         *Cross Multiply*
    2(k-2)=-1(4-x)         *Distribute*
    2k-4= -4+x             *Add 4 to both sides*
    2k=x                   *Divide both sides by k*
    x/k=2

10. **C**; Draw it out and look at the differences between the coordinates of the given point and the midpoint.  To go from (-1,1) to (3,4), the x is increasing by 4 and the y increases by 3.  The change from the midpoint to the endpoint will be the same.  Using the midpoint (3,4) and increasing the x by 4 and the y by 3 gives you the coordinates (7,7).

11. **B**; Draw it out. The shortest distance between two parallel lines is a perpendicular line between them. Both lines have slopes of 1. The slopes cause the lines to form 45 degree angles with the axes. This would form a 45-45-90 right triangle with the y axis forming the hypotenuse. The length of the hypotenuse in this case would be 4 because that is the y intercept of the second line. Therefore, the length of the leg is half of this multiplied by radical 2.

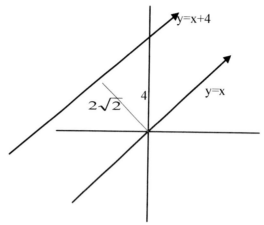

12. **C**; The length of BC is 5. To find the other sides we need to use the distance formula or Pythagorean Theorem If an altitude were dropped from point A to the x axis, its length would be 6. The distance from point B to this point on the x axis is 8. This forms a 6, 8, 10 Pythagorean Triplet. Therefore, AB is 10. To find the length of AC you need to use the distance formula. Point C is at the origin so its coordinates are (0,0).

$$AC = \sqrt{(3-0)^2 + (6-0)^2}$$
$$AC = \sqrt{45} = 3\sqrt{5}$$

Adding the lengths of the sides gives us $5+10+ \ 3\sqrt{5} = 15 + 3\sqrt{5}$

13. **0**; The points (m,n) and (j,k) are the y and x intercepts respectively. This means that m=0 and k=0.

## Pg 119 Quadrilateral and Polygons

1. **145**; Consecutive angles of a parallelogram are supplementary. 35+<B=180 so <B=180.
2. **40**; Know all the properties of the quadrilaterals. Because a rhombus is a parallelogram, the diagonals bisect each other. What makes a rhombus special is that all the sides are equal and the diagonals are perpendicular to each other. When the diagonals are drawn they create 4 congruent right triangles with the sides of the rhombus being the hypotenuses. Use Pythagorean Theorem to find the length of one side and then multiply by 4.

side$^2$=6$^2$+8$^2$
side$^2$=100
side=10

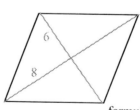

3. **1080**; An octagon has 8 sides. Use the formula
Sum of interior angles=(n-2)180 where n=8
Sum of interior angles=(8-2)(180)=1080

4. **30**; The measure of an exterior angle is 360/n where n represents the number of sides. 360/12=30.
5. **17**; This is a Trojan Horse problem. It looks like a rectangle problem, but you have to know your Pythagorean Triplets. (8, 15, 17)

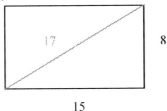

6. **A**; The cutout on the bottom right corner confuses people. If you were to extend the base and the rights sides, it would form a rectangle with an equal perimeter.

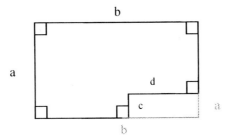

7. **D**; When working with regular (equal sided) polygons of the same area, as the number of sides increase, the length of the sides will decrease. If you need to prove it, draw a square with a side of 10. The area is 100. Using the formula for the area of an equilateral triangle find the length of the side if the area were 100.

$$A = \frac{s^2\sqrt{3}}{4}$$ *Use the formula for the area of an equilateral triangle*

$$100 = \frac{s^2\sqrt{3}}{4}$$ *Let the area be 100. (Area of a square with a side of 10)*

$$400 = s^2\sqrt{3}$$ *Cross multiply*

$$s^2 = \frac{400}{\sqrt{3}}$$ *Solve for the side.*
*Since is is more than 10, we can assume the same will be true*

$$s \approx 15.2$$ *of shapes with more sides*

8. **E**; The area of the circle is $36\pi$, so the radius is 6. Connecting each vertex of the hexagon to its opposite vertex creates 6 equilateral triangle all will a length of 6.

Find the area of a single one of the triangles.

$$A = \frac{s^2\sqrt{3}}{4}$$

$$A = \frac{6^2\sqrt{3}}{4}$$

$$A = 9\sqrt{3}$$

Multiplying this answer by 6 gives us a final answer of $54\sqrt{3}$

9. **C;** After drawing it out, connect E to the midpoint of CD and draw a diagonal to B.

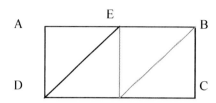

The area of DEBC is 4/5 and this is the area of 3 of the 4 triangles. Set up a proportion to find the area of all 4 of the triangles.

$$\frac{3}{4/5} = \frac{4}{x}$$

$$3x = \frac{16}{5}$$

$$x = 16/15$$

10. **B;** The ratio of the areas and the lengths of the sides of proportional figures will NOT be equal. Take a square with a length of 4. If the sides were increased by 50% they would be 6. The area before and after would be 16 and 36 which reduces to 4:9.
11. **E;** The ratio of the areas will be the ratio of the sides squared. The same rule applies to the diagonals. Squaring the ratio of the diagonals gives us 1:8
12. **36;** A diagonal in a square creates two 45-45-90 right triangles. Since the hypotenuse is 12, the length of the leg is $6\sqrt{2}$. From here, use the formula for the area of a triangle A=1/2 bh.

$$A = \frac{1}{2}(6\sqrt{2})(6\sqrt{2})$$

$$A = \frac{1}{2}(72)$$

$$A = 36$$

13. **18;** The measure of an exterior angle of a regular polygon is 360/n where n is the number of sides. Set up the formula:

| | |
|---|---|
| 20=360/n | *Cross multiply* |
| 20n=360 | *Divide by n* |
| n=18 | |

14. **12;** The area of rectangle ABCD is 48. When the diagonals are drawn 4 triangles with equal areas are created

## Pg.126 Circles

1. **70**; The measure of an inscribed angle is half of its intercepted arc.

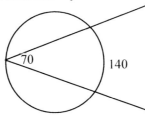

2. **12π**; The area of a circle is found using $A=\pi r^2$. Therefore, the radius is 6 making the diameter 12. The formula for the circumference is $C=\pi d$. The circumference would be 12π.

3. **12.5π**; To find the area of a sector use the formula

$$A = \frac{Angle}{360}(\pi r^2)$$

4. **D**; Since the area if 10π, the radius is the square root of 10. The diameter is twice this length and circumference is equal to π(diamter)

5. **D**; This is a very common "Trojan Horse" question that involves 45-45-90 triangles. Draw a diagram and include an diagonal in the square. The diagonal is the diameter of the circle and the hypotenuse of the 45-45-90 triangle. Since the area of the square is 16, its side will be 4. This means that the hypotenuse is $4\sqrt{2}$ and its radius is $2\sqrt{2}$

6. **E**; The radius is 6 so the diameter is 12 and the circumference will be 12π. A central angle and its intercepted arc have equal measures. $60°$ is 1/6 of $360°$, so the length of the arc will be 5/6 of 12π.

7. **B**; The ratio of the areas will the square of the ratio of the perimeters (circumference). Since the ratio of the areas is 1:2, the ratio of the circumferences will be the square root of this.

8. **D**; The area of the circle is 16π so its radius is 4. A tangent and a radius form a right angle at the point of tangency. Using this and the given fact that angle O is twice angle B, triangle AOB is a 30-60-90 triangle.

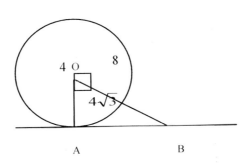

After finding the lengths of the sides, the area of the triangle will be (1/2)(base)(height).

**9. E;** Connecting the centers of each of the circles will form an equilateral triangle with a side of 6. Use the formula for the area of an equilateral triangle:

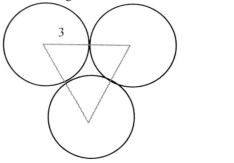

$$A = \frac{s^2 \sqrt{3}}{4}$$

$$A = \frac{6^2 \sqrt{3}}{4}$$

$$A = 9\sqrt{3}$$

Using this information, you would be able to eliminate choices b and d. Now you have to subtract the areas of each of the sectors of the circles. Since the triangle is equilateral, the angles are all 60 degrees. All of the sectors together would form a semicircle (180 degrees) with an area of $9\pi/2$. Subtracting the area of the semicircle from the area of the equilateral triangle gives an area of:

$$9\sqrt{3} - \frac{9\pi}{2}$$

**10. D;** The width of 4 means that the circles have a radius of 2. Using this, the length of the rectangle is 8 and its area is 32. The area of each circle is $4\pi$. The area of the shaded region will be $32-4\pi$.

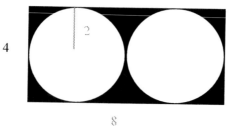

**11. B;** The tangents are perpendicular to the radii. The area of the circle is $4\pi$, so the radius is 2. The measure of angle CBA is 60. Drawing a line connecting points O and B will bisect angles CBA and COB and form two 30-60-90 right triangles. The area of each triangle is $2\sqrt{3}$ so the total area is $4\sqrt{3}$

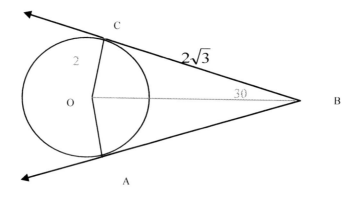

12. **50**; A central angle and its intercepted arc are equal in measure. For this reason, angle AOB is 80. Remember that all radii are equal so this is an isosceles triangle. The two base angles add up to 100 so x=50.

13. **98**; The area of the outer square is 196 so its side is 14. This is also the diameter of the circle and will be diagonal of the inner square. The diagonal of a square forms two 45-45-90 right triangles. Since the diagonal is 14 the side is $7\sqrt{2}$ The area of the square will be 98.

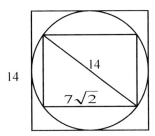

14. **32**; Draw it out but include the diagonal of the square which is also the diameter of the circle. The radius of the square is 4 so the length of the diameter is 8. The diagonal divides the square into two 45-45-90 triangles.

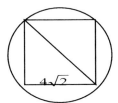

Since the hypotenuse of the triangle is 8 its leg will be $4\sqrt{2}$. Squaring this gives us the area of 32.

15. **120**; Since CO is equal in length to AB, AB is the same length as a radius. This means that triangle AOB is equilateral. All the angles in an equilateral triangle measure 60 degrees an a straight line measures $180^0$. The measure of angle BOC will be 180-60=120.

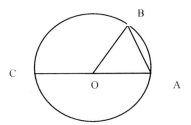

## Pg. 134 Solid Geometry

1. **120 ft$^3$**; The volume of a rectangular prism is found by multiplying the length, width and height.
2. **48π cm$^3$**; The volume of a cylinder is found by using the formula V=π r$^2$h. This formula is given to you on the formula bar at the beginning of each section.
3. **80 cm$^3$**; The volume of any prism is the area of the base multiplied by the height.
4. **C**; The ratio of the volumes is 8:27 so the ratio of the edges is 2:3 (the cube root of 8:27). Since surface area is two dimensional, the ratio of the surface area is (2:3)$^2$ or 4:9.

5. **E;** The distance from the center of the front face to the base and side are each 2. From here use the formula $d^2=l^2+w^2+h^2$

$$d^2=2^2+2^2+4^2$$
$$d^2=24$$
$$d=2\sqrt{6}$$

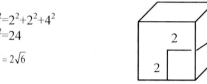

6. **E;** The volume of a cube is found using the formula $V=e^3$ where e is the length of the edge. Since $e^3=8\pi$, a single edge will be the cube root of $8\pi$.

7. **13;** The diagonal of a rectangular prism is found using the formula: $d^2=l^2+w^2+h^2$. This formula is NOT given to you so make sure you know it.

8. **27;** The volume of the cube is 125 so the length of each side is 5. The smaller cubes that are unpainted will be a smaller cube inside the larger cube. The length of each side of the inner cube will be 2 units less than the original cube.

## Pg. 136 Geometry Review

1. **D;** Since it's a right triangle, Pythagorean Theorem can be used.

$$(x+7)^2+(x-7)^2=hyp^2$$
$$x^2+14x+49+x^2-14x+49=hyp^2$$
$$2x^2+98=hyp^2$$

Taking the square root of both sides gives use choice D.

2. **B;** Remember that a the angles along a straight line will add up to 180°. Therefore, 3x=180 and x=60. On the other side of the line we have 4y+x=180. Since x=60, 4y=120 and y=30.

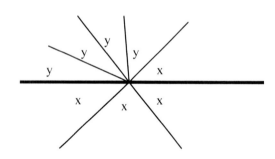

3. **C;** Any two sides of a triangle must add to more than the length of the 3rd side. The most common wrong answer is 4 because people automatically say the sides have lengths of 1, 1, and 2. Not possible since 1+1 is not more than 2. The smallest combination of sides would be 1, 2, and 2.

4. **C;** The ratio of the areas of two similar shapes will be the square of the ratio of the sides. By cutting the perimeter in half, the area would be cut by 1/4.

5. **E;** Any two sides of a triangle must add to more that the 3rd side. Sides of 2, 4, and 6 aren't possible.

6. **B;** The ratio of the perimeters will be the square root of the ratio of the areas.

7. **E;** This question uses a few different angles. The angle adjacent to the 130 must be 50 since a straight line has 180 degrees. This means that the 3rd angle of the triangle must have a measure of 70 since the angles of a triangle also add to 180. The angle x is the alternate interior angle to the 70 degree angle. (You can see the diagram on the following page)

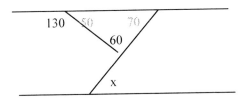

8.  **C;** Use the formula for the area of an equilateral triangle and solve for the side.

$$A = \frac{s^2 \sqrt{3}}{4} \qquad \text{Here's the formula. (KNOW IT)}$$

$$4\sqrt{3} = \frac{s^2 \sqrt{3}}{4} \quad \text{Substitute in the area}$$

$$16\sqrt{3} = s^2 \sqrt{3} \quad \text{Cross multiply}$$

$$s = 4 \qquad \text{Solve for the length of the side}$$

Since the side has a length of 4, the perimeter of the triangle is 12

9.  **C;** This is a classic. Draw out the length the rider traveled. The key to this question is connecting the starting and finishing points and forming a single right triangle. Either use the Pythagorean Theorem or recognize that 5, 12, 13 is a common triplet.

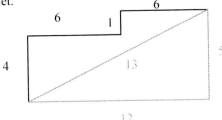

10. **E;** Since it's a rhombus, all the sides are equal. By telling you that AB and BD are both 4, you also know that you have two adjacent equilateral triangles. Use the formula for the area of an equilateral triangle and multiply your final answer by 2.

$$A = \frac{s^2 \sqrt{3}}{4}$$

$$A = \frac{4^2 \sqrt{3}}{4} = 4\sqrt{3}$$

$$2 \; Triangles = 8\sqrt{3}$$

11. **E;** The area of a rectangle is found by A=(length)(width). The length is x, but you don't know what the width is. That is why you are given the diagonal. The diagonal of a rectangle cuts the rectangle into two right triangles. Using the Pythagorean Theorem you would have:

$$10^2 = x^2 + (Width)^2$$

$$100 = x^2 + (Width)^2$$

$$Width^2 = 100 - x^2$$

$$Width = \sqrt{100 - x^2}$$

By solving for the width, now the area could be represented by :

$$A = lw$$

$$A = x\sqrt{100 - x^2}$$

12. **B**; Line AB is parallel to CD and ED is parallel to GF. This means that the measure of angle CDF is equal to the measure of angle ABD because they are corresponding angles. The measure of EDB is equal to the measure of GFD for the same reason. Adding the measures of the two angles (110 and 120) gives us a sum of 230. The overlapping area is angle CDE. Since a straight line has 180 degrees, angle CDE is the difference between 230 and 180 since it was counted twice.

13. **70**; An angle bisector cuts an angle in half. The measure of CBD is 140 because it is a corresponding angle with BDE. This means that the measure of CBA and ABD are both 70. Angle BAD is the alternate interior angle to CBA.

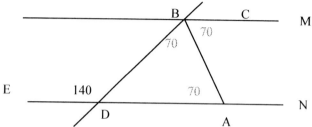

14. **140**; The interior angle is always the supplement of the exterior angle.

15. **1/2 or .5**; Start with a square with sides of 10(you can randomly pick any number) and draw a circle inside. The circle will have a diameter of 10 and a radius of 5. Now, draw a square inside the circle. It's a little more difficult to find the length of the square. You have to draw a diagonal forming two 45-45-90 right triangles.

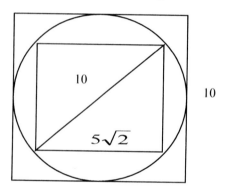

The diagonal of the interior square will also be a diameter, so the length will be 10. Using the rules for the 45-45-90 triangle, the side of the square will have a length of $5\sqrt{2}$
The area of a square can be found by squaring the length of the sides. Therefore, the area of the inside square is 50 and the outside square is 100.

# Appendix B:  Formula Sheets

# SAT Formulas

It's the night/week before the test and your wondering what to study. These are the formulas you NEED to know. The simplest facts have been left out (operations with integers shouldn't be an issue at this point). These are the facts that people have trouble with.

## Arithmetic Facts

Prime Number: A number divisible only by one and itself. 2 is the smallest prime number and is the ONLY even prime.

### Even and Odd Facts (only integers are even or odd)

| | |
|---|---|
| E+E=E | E*E=E |
| O+O=E | O*O=O |
| E+O=O | E*O=E |

Remember that there is no rule for division!

Zero is an Even number

$(Negative)^{Even}$=Positive
$(Negative)^{Odd}$=Negative

If x>y then, -x<-y. When you multiply or divide by a negative number, switch the inequality.

### Absolute Value

$|x - h| = c$
    reads "x is a number c units from h"

## Functions

A function passes the vertical line test.
X= domain         Y=range

### Transformations of Functions

-f(x): reflection in x axis
F(-x): reflection in y axis
F(x)+k: vertical shift of k units
F(x+h): horizontal shift of –h units. Remember, the horizontal shift goes in the opposite direction of the sign

## Algebra Facts

### Exponent/Radical Rules

1. $(x^a)(x^b)=x^{a+b}$
2. $(x^a)^b=x^{ab}$
3. $\dfrac{x^a}{x^b} = x^{a-b}$
4. $x^0=1$
5. $x^1=x$
6. $x^{-1}=1/x$
7. $(x^a)(y^a)=(xy)^a$
8. $(\sqrt{x})(\sqrt{y})= \sqrt{xy}$
9. $\sqrt{x} + \sqrt{y} \neq \sqrt{x+y}$
10. $\sqrt{\dfrac{x}{y}} = \dfrac{\sqrt{x}}{\sqrt{y}}$
11. $\sqrt[a]{x^b} = x^{\frac{b}{a}}$

### Special Factors

1. $x^2-y^2=(x+y)(x-y)$
2. $(x+y)^2=x^2+2xy+y^2$
3. $(x-y)^2=x^2-2xy+y^2$

Trap!! $(x^2+y^2)$ doesn't factor!

### Rational Expressions

$\dfrac{x+y}{x+y} = 1$

$\dfrac{x-y}{y-x} = -1$

$\dfrac{x+y}{x-y} = Doesn"t\ Simplify$

## Fractions/Ratios/Percentages

Fraction=Part/Whole          Ratio=Part/Part

If x/y is a ratio, then x/(x+y) is the fraction.

If $0<x<1$, then $x^2<x<\sqrt{x}$ (the higher the exponent, the lower the number)

### Percentage Yo-Yo Trap!
Changing up, then down (or down, then up) by the same percentage will NEVER give you the same number. You will always end up with a little less that what you started with.

200% of a number is 2 times the number.
300% of a number is 3 times the number.

Percentage Change=(change/original)*100%

## Sequences
An arithmetic sequence is one where you add a common difference (d) to find each successive term. To find the nth term use the formula:
$$A_n=a_1+d(n-1)$$

A geometric sequence is where you multiply by a common term (r) to find each successive term. To find the nth term use the formula:
$$A_n=a_1r^{n-1}$$

## Average/Statistics

Mean=average
Median=middle
Mode=most frequently occurring

For a set of data, the total deviation above the average=the total deviation below the mean.

For a set of consecutive numbers, the mean will equal the median.

If a question requires you to compare two averages, use the diagram below to organize your information

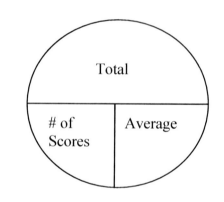

| Line and Angle Facts | Triangle Facts |
|---|---|
| **Line and Angle Facts**<br><br>A straight line has 180 degrees.<br><br>The sum of the angles around a point is 180°.<br><br>Vertical Angles are congruent.<br><br>Know all the angles formed parallel lines cut by a transversal. Any set of two angles will either be congruent or supplementary. | **Triangle Facts**<br><br>The sum of the angles is 180°.<br><br>Any two sides of a triangle must add to more than the length of the 3rd side.<br><br>An isosceles triangle has two equal sides and two equal base angles.<br><br>In an isosceles triangle, the altitude drawn to the base, will bisect the base and the vertex angle.<br><br>An equilateral triangle has 3 equal sides. All of the angles measure 60°. |
| **Quadrilaterals/Polygons/Circles**<br><br>The sum of the angles in a quadrilateral is 360.<br><br>The sum of the interior angles of ANY polygon with n sides is (n-2)180. To find the measure of a single interior angle divide this number by n.<br><br>The sum of the exterior angles of any polygon is 360.<br><br>Exterior angle=360/n<br><br>A regular polygon has equal sides and angles.<br><br>A diagonal in a square creates 2 isosceles right triangles.<br><br>All radii in a circle are equal.<br><br>A radius will form a right angle with a tangent when they meet.<br><br>The ratio of the areas of two similar polygons will be the square of the ratio of the sides.<br>Ex. 1:3(sides)è1:9(area) | The area of a triangle=1/2 bh<br><br>Area of an equilateral triangle= $\dfrac{s^2\sqrt{3}}{4}$<br><br>Pythagorean Theorem: $a^2+b^2=c^2$<br><br>Triplets:  3,  4,  5<br>5, 12, 13<br>7, 24, 25<br>8, 15, 17<br><br>The multiples of a triplet will also work  (ex 6, 8,10)<br><br>**Special Right Triangles**<br>The sides of a 30:60:90 triangle are in a ratio of x: $x\sqrt{3}$ :2x.<br><br>The sides of a 45:45:90 triangle are in a ratio of x:x: $x\sqrt{2}$ . If you are given the hypotenuse as a whole number, then use the ratio $\dfrac{x\sqrt{2}}{2} : \dfrac{x\sqrt{2}}{2} : x$ |

## Coordinate Geometry

Slope: $\dfrac{y_2 - y_1}{x_2 - x_1}$

Midpoint: $\left( \dfrac{x_1 + x_2}{2}, \dfrac{y_1 + y_2}{2} \right)$

Distance: $\sqrt{(x_1 - x_2)^2 + (y_1 - y_2)^2}$

The distance formula will often involve Pythagorean Triplets. Make sure you know them.

The slopes of parallel lines are equal.
The slopes of perpendicular lines are negative reciprocals.

Horizontal lines have a slope of Zero
Vertical Lines have no slope (undefined).

Given a line in the form y=mx+b form, the m is equal to the slope and the b is the y intercept.

The slope of any line going through the origin and a point (x,y) will be y/x.

## Solid Geometry

The volume of a cube with edge, e, is $e^3$.

The surface area of a cube is $6e^2$

The volume of two similar prisms will be the ratio of their corresponding edges raised to the 3rd power.
Ex. 1:3(sides) 1:27(volumes)

The volume of a cylinder is $V=\pi r^2 h$

In a rectangular prism, the length of the diagonal going through the prism can be found using the equation
$D^2 = l^2 + w^2 + h^2$